Foreword

This book gathers direct voices from Ukraine. People describe destroyed homes, forced displacement, captivity, and survival. They speak with precision, leaving no space for interpretation other than the truth of what happened.

Each testimony is evidence. It records events as they unfolded, names those who endured them, and preserves the memory of those who did not return. Together they create a record that resists distortion and erasure.

In Management in Times of War I reflected on how institutions and leaders operated under extreme pressure. This book preserves another layer: the everyday voices of people who endured the same war from basements, occupied streets, and prison cells. Both perspectives form a broader picture of how Ukraine withstood the invasion—at the level of state and at the level of individual lives.

For the reader, these pages offer a framework to recognise patterns of violence and resilience, and to carry this knowledge into judgment and action.

Kostiantyn Koshelenko
Author of *Management in Times of War* and *Leadership in Times of War*
Former Deputy Minister of Social Policy of Ukraine

Introduction

Since we all live in a diverse world and are bombarded by information, it is only natural that something very important might not get our attention. The reason we have created this book is to show you something that is already on our doorstep and hopefully will never reach your neighbourhood: the Russian Peace, or Russkiy Mir.

Consolidation of the 'Russkiy Mir' is key to Russia's war aims. It is usually translated as 'the Russian World', an imperialistic concept involving the unification of all Russian language speakers, believed to be an integral part of the Russian community reflecting their common history and culture. However, the principal meaning of the word 'Mir' is 'Peace' (readers might remember the Soviet space station was named Mir) and so to a Russian speaker Russkiy Mir is also Russian Peace, a strange concept of peace, an authoritarian peace imposed by cruelty and force.

Our mission is to tell true stories and to encourage you to explore more. The information is there, in the open, but unfortunately most of it slips through the cracks. To understand the Russian Peace, you have to go to the source. To see how from the earliest age children in Russia now are being prepared to fight and die. Starting from the maternity ward, where they may be discharged dressed in military blankets resembling those of the Second World War, to nursery, where every 9th of May preschoolers perform death scenes and military parades, to the training of adolescents in contemporary youth militant organisations—everything prepares them for a future based entirely on a glorified Soviet version of the past.

While most countries rethink their colonial history and reflect on their mistakes, the idea of the Russian Peace is to glorify that past and physically destroy everyone who doesn't agree. No wonder that their worst tyrants have come back to life: new monuments to Stalin are erected, including in a Moscow Metro station, and people bring flowers and openly worship that maniac, a man responsible for the death of millions. In the occupied territories, military and detention camps are being established, and by the time the children trained in these camps reach adulthood, they will be prepared to inflict the same cruelty they themselves have endured and been taught.

Given that this system shows no mercy even to its own people and fosters a cult of violence and death, it is hardly surprising that 93% of Ukrainians in captivity are subjected to torture. Cruelty is not merely a by-product of war; it is embedded

UKRAINIAN WAR STORIES

Compiled by
Jenny Carr & Nadiia Karpenko

Helion & Company Limited

Helion & Company Limited
Unit 8 Amherst Business Centre
Budbrooke Road
Warwick
CV34 5WE
UK
Tel. 01926 499619
Email: info@helion.co.uk
Website: www.helion.co.uk
X (formerly Twitter): @Helionbooks
Facebook: @HelionBooks
Visit our blog at https://helionbooks.wordpress.com/

Undergroundstrategy UK, 15a Mansionhouse Road, Edinburgh, EH9 1TZ, UK/
Undergroundstrategy USA, 303 Division LLC, 120 E Grand Ave, Suite 121, Clovis, NM
88101, USA

Co-published by Helion & Company & Undergroundstrategy 2025
Designed and typeset by Mach 3 Solutions (www.mach3solutions.co.uk)
Front cover by Max Lauker, One Ping Only, onepingonly.io
Text © Jenny Carr and Nadiia Karpenko 2025

ISBN 978-1-804519-15-8

British Library Cataloguing-in-Publication Data.
A catalogue record for this book is available from the British Library.

For details of other military history titles published by Helion & Company Limited,
contact the above address, or visit our website: http://www.helion.co.uk

We always welcome receiving book proposals from prospective authors.

Contents

Underground Strategy Press— Helion

As series editors, we are delighted to introduce the Underground Strategy Press— Helion series. Our goal is to publish life-writing that reimagines the ways in which personal and historical narratives intersect. Memoir, biography, reflection—each volume in this series is chosen for its originality of voice and perspective.

In commissioning works for Underground Strategy—Helion, we look for authors who bring a deeply personal lens to their subjects: war, conflict, leadership, loss, identity, memory. We seek writing that takes risks.

This series is not constrained by period, region, or genre. We welcome the unexpected—voices from outside the usual canon, stories not yet told, perspectives not yet considered. Whether dealing with the trenches, post-conflict society, the inner life of an individual, or the quiet work of remembrance, each book aims to illuminate something new.

Tony Garcia and Max Lauker
Series Editors

in the shifting chimera of ideology that dehumanises the enemies of the system, such as the Ukrainians who fight for independence and who reject the so-called Russian Peace.

We have compiled true stories from a wide range of people—accounts so horrific that they may seem almost unimaginable. It is vital for humanity to recognise that no justification exists for such cruelty, and speaking out is the first step in confronting it.

The book is divided into four main sections: refugees, people in captivity, life in the occupied territories, and a final section titled *'Civilians and Soldiers'*. Some accounts are narrated in the first person, others in the third. A few are drawn from direct interviews; most are based on reports and interviews published in the Ukrainian press, with the principal sources listed at the end of each piece. All cited media outlets have been informed, and permission to publish our adaptations has been requested. Some accounts contain graphic and distressing material. Reader discretion is advised.

N

RUSSIA

Chernihiv
Lukashivka

Chernivtsi

Sumy

Sumy

Hostomel
Bucha
Kyiv
Kotsybinsk

Kyiv

Valuyki

Kharkiv

Poltava

Kharkiv

Poltava

Borova

Luhansk

Cherkasy

Sievierodonetsk

Lysychansk
Schastya

Kropyvnytskyi

Kirovohrad

Dnipro

Dnipropetrovsk

Bakhmut
Chasiv Yar
Radynske
Yasynuvata
Marinka
Olenivka

Myrnograd
Donetsk

Luhansk

Kryvyi Rih

Zaporizhzhia

Zaporizhzhia

Donetsk

Mykolaiv

Pavlopil

Odesa
Mykolaiv

Melitopol

Dmytrivka

Mariupol

Chornobaevka
Kakhovka
Oleshky

Berdyansk

Odesa
Kherson
Skadovsk

Kherson

Sea of
Azov

Zalizny Port

Black Sea

Crimea
Simferopol

Sevastopol
Sevastopol

Map of Ukraine showing the cities and town mentioned in the book.

Section Introduction: Refugees

At 5am Ukrainian time on Thursday 24 February 2022 Putin appeared on television with the stark announcement 'I have decided on a military operation'. At the same time there were reports of explosions in Kyiv and Mariupol. Very soon these reports were coming in thick and fast as it became clear that Russia had launched a full-scale invasion with bombs and troops pouring into Ukraine across all its borders.

On that morning Ukrainians had been woken by sirens and by the phone calls of friends with the news that everyone had dreaded and yet not imagined possible.

In fact, the Russians had been massing troops across the border for months and there had been other ominous signs of the impending invasion in recent days such as their build-up of blood supplies (which we learned about later). Although United States (US) intelligence and others had warned for months of an impending invasion, many—in Ukraine and abroad, including it seems the Ukrainian government—struggled to believe it, leaving the population unprepared. When reality struck on the 24th, citizens began making Molotov cocktails, and the government declared martial law.

The stories in the following section were written by people from cities across Ukraine which have subsequently seen horrors unimaginable—including the atrocities committed in Bucha, Mariupol and Kherson. They describe the shock of invasion and their attempts to do the best for their families. The writers were soon refugees outside Ukraine. Names have been changed but the stories are in their words.

Happy Story

My name is Maria or Mary in English. I am a mum, and we are from Mariupol, the city in Ukraine that suffered immense destruction by Russia in 2022 and is currently occupied. Mariupol defended itself against Russian occupying forces and won the fight in 2014 and we were sure that Mariupol would now hold out as well.

On the 24th February 2022, not considering the situation to be serious, we took our young child to nursery and went to work. Literally within an hour, the air defence system sirens wailed and the nursery teacher called us to say that all children were being taken to a bomb shelter. From that moment onwards our life turned upside down. Under the air raid sirens, I ran out of my office (which was right in the centre of Mariupol, near the Drama Theatre and the National Security Service of Ukraine (SBU)) and rushed to the nursery to collect my daughter and take her home. We ran home, gathered items and documents and rushed to my parents' house in the suburbs which had a basement. We sought cover and protection there for seven days and somehow, we survived. On 2 March, one week later, we lost energy and water supplies and had no means of communication; worse was still to come. We had only small food rations and a water container to survive on and firewood to keep us warm. Before long, the water ran out and we had to rely on melting snow, gathering rainwater and water from the valley.

With every passing day, the explosions of artillery shells were coming closer and closer to our home. From our window on the second floor of my father's house, we could see high rise residential buildings in the centre of Mariupol being attacked and consumed by fire. My father and my husband would go down together to the valley to fetch water. The stories that they shared with us were truly horrifying. They witnessed a lot of dead bodies, people who had been shot near to the well.

On 6 March, the sounds of attack were deafening. A bombshell landed in our courtyard. Our car was badly damaged and half of our neighbour's house was blown away but luckily we all somehow survived. We remained in the basement in fear of our lives.

On 15 March, we heard rumours that seemingly the Russian soldiers were allowing civilians out of Mariupol city. Collecting the bare necessities, we got in our car that had no glass in the window frames and no windscreen. The weather conditions in Mariupol at that time of year were below 0 degrees Celsius.

Leaving Mariupol city, travelling in the direction of Berdyansk city, we passed through 15 checkpoints of the Russian army. During 8 hours of car travel, we managed to cover only 70 km (43 miles). At each checkpoint, the men wore masks and had machine guns and would demand to check our documents.

Reaching Dmytrivka village in the Berdyansk region, we were not allowed to go on to the checkpoint because of the curfew and so we had to turn back and go to a nearby village. Luckily, there was a school in the village where they housed fleeing

Mariupol residents. We were persuaded to stay there for protection. We agreed because the temperature outside was freezing and our car had no glass windows; it was impossible to go further with a young child. Despite all of this we remained hopeful that the invasion would end soon and Mariupol would again be a part of Ukraine.

An entire month passed and we finally had the courage to leave the village and continue our escape through the only remaining safe corridor via Crimea.

Upon approaching the Border crossing, we had to wait in a long line and then we were all interrogated for 24 hours including my four-year-old daughter. We were finally released. A few days later, we managed to reach the border with Estonia. From there we continued to travel through Europe to be reunited with friends in the United Kingdom (UK).

I believe that my story is a happy story, we escaped, we survived. Praise the Lord for that. None of my loved ones died. But I know dozens of tragic stories of my friends and relatives. We believe in our victory! Glory to Ukraine!

Seventeen to sixty

My name is Sofia. I am originally from Kherson, Ukraine and I've been in the UK since April 2022.

The population of Kherson before the occupation was roughly 300,000 and it has been reduced to 2% of that now. And regrettably it is still reducing due to constant missile attacks taking the lives of civilians.

Here is my story of what I witnessed first-hand in Russian occupied Kherson.

On the 24th of February 2022 I woke up early, very early, one morning, you might even say at night, startled by the menacing sounds in the distance. At that moment, I wasn't aware that Russian troops had already entered Ukraine and were driving through villages in tanks and armoured vehicles shooting innocent and peaceful civilians. They began destroying and killing everything and everyone in sight.

Russian troops had already captured the roads leading to and from Kherson. They hadn't entered the city of Kherson yet but escaping from the city was already close to impossible! Some families made their attempt at escape that day, despite this, hoping for the best. They tried to get through the checkpoints of the Russians in their cars. Later we found out they had been shot dead by the Russian forces and mercenaries on the roads of the Kherson region!

On March 1st Russian troops entered Kherson city. The courageous Kherson men stood up to defend their families and their native city. But what chance did they have? Several months before the invasion the so-called head of the local administration ordered civilians to surrender anything that could be used as weapons such as hunting weapons or any other kind of weapons. As a matter of fact, we faced the armed Russian army barehanded. We were rendered helpless in front of this gigantic monster! What weapons could our men have? Some created homemade explosives to defend themselves, their families and their communities. All those who stood up against the aggression were shot dead by the war tanks. All of them who came to defend Kherson. The youngest was 17 and the oldest was 60. With that in mind, now you can understand the title of this story to honour our selfless, brave and courageous defenders.

The very same day, March 1st, the Russian occupiers were driving their tanks along Kherson streets firing at residential houses. Our house was one of the first they fired at. The balcony of one of our neighbours collapsed to the ground. The building was shaking. Some people were injured. My darling daughter fell to the floor and covered her head with her hands. I just froze on the spot and continued to stand. The entire world collapsed for us at that moment! Russia began the genocide of Ukrainians. They have taken away everything from us: our freedom, our right to exist, our land and our future. My life disappeared overnight when I lost my home, my Kherson…

The Russian occupiers were driving around the streets of Kherson shooting all those they didn't 'like' for this or that reason. And then they didn't allow people to take the dead bodies of their loved ones! There was blood on the walls of the buildings and pavements. We lived under Russian occupation for 25 days! I would never wish anyone to live a single day under Russian occupation!

My family managed to leave Kherson! On the 3rd attempt! Yes, we were lucky! We managed to survive.

But for all those who were killed, the perpetrators should face justice and be brought to trial! They have to be held responsible for all the terror! They have to pay for the death of every single person! For destroying the health of every single person! For every single ruined building! For every single pet killed!

I would also like to express my gratitude to the people of Scotland for rendering us help, providing us with everything necessary and keeping us safe. Our lives would have been drastically different if not for you.

I am really sorry that I am old and perhaps won't see my homeland again, with my own eyes within my lifetime. I feel a strong desire for my daughter to return to Ukraine, and witness those who have wronged our people brought to justice.

My dream is for Ukraine to be triumphant and victorious.

Ukraine, our country of marigolds, sunflowers and wheatfields. We will be forever proud to be Ukrainian people.

The Occupation of Kherson

From the very first days of the war my daughter would go to a bomb shelter during the air raids. It was not a specially built bomb shelter but was rather the basement in the building of the Institute for Teachers' Refresher Courses. The Institute was located right opposite our apartment. It does not exist at the moment as it was destroyed during the shelling. But at the beginning of the war, it was still there, and people would go to its basement to hide from the shelling. The basement was not big enough for everyone who tried to find refuge, so animals were not allowed in. We had a big dog who had to stay with me at our flat during the shelling. But to tell you the truth it was not safe in that basement either as in the worst scenario, in case the building was damaged and collapsed, it would bury everyone seeking shelter. My daughter and some other people understood that so they would not go down to the basement but would stay on the ground floor believing that it would be easier to reach them if the building collapsed.

During the very first days of the Russian occupation of Kherson people were desperate to get whatever they could get in the shops and pharmacies. There were enormous queues at every shop. People were buying whatever they could. There were very long queues at the ATM machines too as people were trying to withdraw their money. In a couple of days all the shop shelves were absolutely empty. Nothing was left. Though one day I found vinegar in one of the shops and was immensely happy as I knew that you could use vinegar to lower high blood pressure. As pharmacies could not offer the medication people needed it was important to use so-called traditional methods to fight their health problems. But soon the Ukrainian currency was devalued to such an extent that it was like toy money. And when the invaders introduced their Russian roubles, Ukrainian money became completely useless.

When the Russians captured the Kherson region not only were people left without food supplies but animals too. There is a village called Chornobaevka not far from Kherson which had the biggest poultry farm in Europe. Their chickens were sold all over Ukraine and even abroad. There was no food to feed those chickens. The Russian occupiers starved those poor chickens to death. They ordered the workers from the poultry farm to stay away from the farm and not to bring food to the chickens. Later vans from Chornobaevka were driving around Kherson giving away chickens to people. Those were the chickens who died from starvation. They were very thin. For the first time in my adult life, I was plucking chickens and then storing them in the freezer. Only now I have found out that more than 4.4 million chickens died of hunger at the Chornobaevka poultry farm. Plus, there was no ventilation because there was no electricity. We now call it ecocide. The Russian occupiers said that lorries with mixed feed were interfering with the movement of the Russian military on the highway. At the moment Chornobaevka is liberated but because of the destruction and mining of the fields there are no jobs and only 5 per cent of the agricultural land can be used.

During the occupation of Kherson people talked about two snipers who would choose a roof of the building in any district of Kherson and would start shooting whoever they wanted to shoot. The worst thing was you could never know which roof they would choose and who would become the victims of their entertainment.

Bucha Story

On the 24th of February 2022 I was woken up at 4:45 am by Maksym, my husband, who told me that war had broken out. At that moment I was on sick leave and our children were staying with their grannies. Kateryna was in Bucha while Artem and Viktoria were in Vynogradar, a district of Kyiv. Getting dressed in a matter of minutes we jumped in our car. Then filled it at the filling station. We called mum asking her to wake Kateryna. Arriving at our flat in Bucha I embraced my mum and dad, took Kateryna and we set off for Vynogradar to pick up our other two children. Then we saw enormous lines at the filling stations. It was a good thing that we already had a full tank of petrol. We picked up our children from Vynogradar but we could not drive home. We had to leave the car, and it took us an hour to get home to Kyiv.

At the same time my parents took all their documents and moved from their flat to their dacha on the outskirts of Bucha, close to Hostomel.[1] From there you could get a good view of Hostomel Airport and the servicemen's buildings. At that time we did not know yet that real hell would come to that place soon.

There were air raids in Bucha on the 24th of February, at the very beginning of the war. And on the 26th of February Russian troops entered Bucha. My mum and dad helped to hide two men from a territorial defence team during the night of the 25th to the 26th of February. At dawn they left their hiding place and started in the direction of Kyiv and in a few hours the Russian occupiers became 'masters' of Bucha.

From time to time my dad would visit their flat in Bucha to get some drinking water because there was none at the dacha, which is located near the Warsaw highway. Their block of flats had been shelled and the roof was burnt down as well as two entrances to the block. Our kitchen had been sprayed with machine gun bullets. At that moment it still existed though it was destroyed later. Because my dad often commuted between the dacha and the flat, he saw a lot of Russian soldiers and the Russians saw him. He was stopped by the Russians and warned not to come

---

1   A dacha is a country house or cottage, typically used as a seasonal or weekend retreat.

back. And they also sent a message to their checkpoints 'Don't allow that limping man to pass through.' And their checkpoints were everywhere. So my dad had to stop visiting their flat in Bucha.

On the 28th of February mobile phone reception was blocked, and there was no internet connection either. In order to call us my dad had to climb a hill. He tried to tell me where the checkpoints of the Russian occupiers were located. But again, the connection was very poor. I asked him to find a better signal, but he did not understand me and anyway it was impossible to do. On one occasion, as he was returning after these attempted calls to us, he was arrested by two Russian officers—one an ethnic Russian and the other a Buryat.[2] All the rest were sitting on the APC (armoured personnel carrier). They ordered my father to kneel down and to speak Russian. My father refused to do either. Then they hit him between the shoulder blades with a machine gun and made him kneel. All of them were wearing balaclavas so my father could not see their faces. Then they put the barrel of the gun to the back of his head and told him that they were going to shoot him right there. Then my father said to them: 'Who would you rather deal with—a traitor or a patriot? This is my land, I live here, and what are you doing here?' I don't know which language he used to say all this, Ukrainian or Russian, but they ordered him to stand up and lead them to his house.

Our dacha is located right at the far end of the dacha cooperative and borders on a field on one side. My father was led to the dacha by the two Russians. The others were driving in their APC following them. When my mother saw the Russians holding their machine guns at my father's head leading him to his house, she covered her eyes with her hands. While my father was interrogated by the officer, the Buryat man was standing next to my mother. And he was staring at our house. Then my mother asked him 'Why are you staring at my house?'. 'You are living so well here' was his surprised answer. At that time the other Russians, those who were in the APC, started searching our house, turning everything upside down. My dad realised that they were looking for Ukrainian patriotic symbols, military uniform or something like that. The only symbol that we had was our Ukrainian Trident carved on one of the walls of our house. But they either did not recognise it or did not know anything about the Trident. They were searching everywhere, our house, our pantry, our cellar. They could not find anything so they left saying, 'Don't interfere.' They searched every house in this way and if the house was locked and the owners had left, they would break down the door. This all happened at the beginning of March, I can't tell you the exact dates. During all those days there was constant shelling, gunfire, and missiles hitting the ground. The explosions could be heard from near and far. After dark the shelling turned the night into bright morning.

---

2   A Buryat is a member of the Buryat people, an indigenous ethnic group native to Siberia, mainly living around Lake Baikal in Russia.

The next day my dad called me to say that there was an evacuation column being organised in front of the Town Hall. They took everything they needed and left. It was the only evacuation column that did not come under fire. At the checkpoint the Russians found a Ukrainian flag in the glove box of the car. My parents had forgotten about it. The Russians trampled on our flag with their feet. They cursed my parents with all possible swear words but luckily, they allowed the car to pass.

On the 7th of March my parents reached Italy and when Bucha was liberated from the Russian occupiers they returned. I could send you a video of our flat. There is one thing I would like to tell you—everything that was made of glass was broken to pieces, everything made of wood like doors, or plinths was broken or pulled out. Our TV and the children's toys were taken away. My mom cries every time she enters her flat though one year and a half has passed since they came back. She says it would be easier for her if it was all burned down. Now she feels as if 'all her life was raped by Russians.'

The Main Thing is that we are Alive

I want to share with you how I experienced war without even shooting a single bullet.

The situation in Kyiv during the first days of the Russian war against Ukraine was really very tense.

Particularly the wailing of air raid sirens and sprints to the nearest bomb shelter (actually a nearby multi-storey car park). On the third day of the invasion, we made a decision in our family council to leave Kyiv and to go to our house in the countryside which would be safer and more secure for our family. I (the father of the family) planned to return to Kyiv to help support the country's territorial defence team.

So we started off and had to detour some 110 km (68.4 miles). The journey would usually take three times less time. However, with some moral tension and wondering if we were doing the right thing, we managed to reach our village.

For the first two days, it was nice and comfortable and we had fast internet. There is beautiful nature all around our house. You could describe our village as a one-horse town with lots of marshes and no proper road coming through it, unlike many elite 'dacha villages' for the Soviet political elite with their golf courses, outdoor swimming pools and hunting grounds. It was a very basic former Soviet-era dacha (holiday house) cooperative set beside forested hills and wild fields. It is located in between two international motorways and that turned out to be extremely dangerous.

At the end of the second day we had a total blackout with no electricity, no gas and no internet connection. Our only modern convenience was a generator that we could use for not more than one hour twice a day, to warm the house, cook food and charge mobile phones. Our communication with the outside world came to an abrupt end.

On the third night missiles started to fly above our dacha, then Russian military aeroplanes. Our Ukrainian forces started to shoot them down and I was very relieved and happy about that. Honestly! However, when the debris started to fall on our heads it was no laughing matter. Debris was falling on our yard and set fire to the forest. The missiles that were intended for Kyiv were falling all around us. Our missile defence system was clearly working effectively in preventing Russian missiles hitting the capital. The missile bombardment and air raids intensified from then on. The attacks were usually either at night or in the early hours of the morning. The air raid sirens were in Kyiv but here the sirens were the explosions. During one hit, our house shook violently, and our courtyard was showered with something very fine and metallic. Then on the 4th or 5th day an aviation bomb fell on our neighbour's house. Everything was consumed by fire together with the neighbour himself. Then we were fired at with mortars by the Russian forces. Sadly, another neighbour was killed.

Russian helicopters were flying over our valley, enemy helicopters K 50s, K 52s and Mi 8s. All of them were grey like the plague. They seemed so near you could almost touch them. And what was the most painful thing was there was no way of us reporting these enemy assaults as all communication networks had been wiped out. You can imagine our feeling of helplessness and anger. There are many words to describe these Russian Orcs, and I am sure you can all imagine the strong four-letter words that might be used.

The days got mixed up and the hours too. On the sixth day our home was utterly frozen. It was the middle of winter when temperatures can go as low as -10 degrees Celsius. We would switch on our generator only for one hour each day to cook food and to try to keep us warm. When there were air raids, we slept in the basement with the temperature approximately 5 degrees Celsius. This lasted for seven days. We listed all our food rations on a piece of paper, including cat food. It was very difficult to calm our 5-year-old child down and to entertain him. He couldn't understand what was going on. And then he started to guess.

The last four days, there were artillery battles with tanks and infantry. Presumably the missiles had run out. Aviation as well was a rare phenomenon. There was firing everywhere and from everywhere. It was not clear from whom or from where. Civilians who tried to drive on the Zhytomyr motorway were shot dead.

My wife Kateryna was quite euphoric and elevated at the beginning. Then her cheerful mood melted away and became negative. Our son sensed it all and we did not see him smile for days. There was only apathy and complete indifference. But when our boy began to imitate the Kyiv air raid sirens and comment on the bomb explosions, I realised that something had to be done very urgently. I didn't want my son to remember these war sounds, but of course it will stay with him.

All day long we had to wear warm outdoor clothes in case of an urgent need to run somewhere. It was heavy to wear something you would usually wear outdoors in winter. To sleep in those clothes. To live in them day after day. And to get used to the unnatural sounds of exploding bombs and missiles was difficult, particularly for our young son.

Evacuation columns were formed in the villages. Although information about them seldom reached us as we were not from any of those villages but belonged to the dacha cooperative. As a result we did not leave.

During the last days of our dacha stay, we managed to contact friends from a historical reconstruction group who helped us to find volunteers from the evacuation columns. It was hard to get started with the evacuation. Having got together with neighbours who owned cars, we decided to wait for the volunteer guide who could lead us out. However, we were not able to make contact with the volunteers for quite a long time. We were desperate and didn't know what to do. Then very heavy shelling started all around us from tanks and artillery. The Russian Orcs were attacking our military units from every direction. While this hell that was going on, we made the decision to get in the cars and start moving away from the cooperative back to Kyiv.

I don't know what route we took as our neighbours in their car were leading the way. Some kind of fields, some kind of crossings. There were broken power lines everywhere. Somewhere on the horizon, we could see black smoke. In one place, a Russian Armoured Personnel Carrier opened up a merciless barrage on us. It was absolutely terrifying. We had to speed up. The main thing was to get as far away from Zhytomyr motorway as possible. We had white flags, with signs saying 'Children'. We were moving slowly in a column. But the Russian Orcs couldn't care less. We broke through. Alive. And finally back home in Kyiv.

In conclusion,

- Famine is a terrible thing particularly if you have a 5-year-old child and have to explain that you have only what is in your hands to feed them, this is really painful.

- I made a decision, important and adequate for that moment but I will always regret it. I thought we would be safe in our country dacha, which nearly turned out to be a fatal mistake.

- I lost 5 kg.

- My beloved wife has a new, enforced, hairstyle because of stress hair loss and no washing facilities. I am a pretty bad hairdresser.

- I can distinguish by ear the fire from a tank, guns of different calibres, and Grad rockets (multiple rocket launcher system), aviation bombs and all the instruments of pain, suffering and death. The sounds of helicopters, all kinds of drones, bayraktars, aeroplanes as well as the direction of their flight. When Pion guns are in action, the house shakes severely.

- When Grad rockets are fired over the forest they set fire to the tops of the trees due to their reactive trace.

- Adults occasionally behave like children. They are sometimes inadequate when they need to concentrate, to gather their courage and make the right quick decision.

- Kyiv air raid sirens are not as scary as the debris that is falling on your head.

- The suburbs in some cases are not as safe as a big city.

- The main goal for civilians is not to hang around where you are not supposed to be and please don't interfere with the work of our military to destroy the enemy. Listen to the air raid warnings. Stay in the bomb shelter. New iron will be forged and new bricks will be laid. But your life is precious. Nothing will substitute it.

- When we were leaving Kyiv, it was as if it was just starting to wake up and defend itself. When we came back, Kyiv was a fortress.

- It's a pity that our neighbour, Belarus, is so unconditionally supportive of Russia in destroying Ukraine and all our people. It appears that the majority of Belarusians tolerate this. They downplay and deny all the destruction and losses of civilians perpetrated by the occupying Russian forces.

Russia's ongoing onslaught is sweeping everything away, no mercy, no green corridors, no supply of food and energy. That is evil incarnate. They are strong. They are liars, they are cunning, they are very dangerous. They don't have God on their side as they claim, otherwise those things wouldn't happen. They worship death, torture and destruction. They are thirsty for blood and to destroy Ukraine and its peaceful people.

We hold Russia responsible for every lost life, for every lost future! We will overcome!

Section Introduction: Captivity

No one would argue that prisoners of war are among the most vulnerable categories of people, as their lives, health and sanity depend entirely on the goodwill of their captors. Despite the existence of numerous international regulations, in the case of Russia, none are being enforced. The dire health of Ukrainian defenders and civilians in captivity—when measured against the standards of the Geneva Convention—serves as clear evidence of the inhumane conditions and torture they have endured in prisons and camps scattered across the vast territory of the Russian Federation.'

The United Nations (UN) High Commissioner for Human Rights, Volker Türk, warned of the widespread and systematic torture of Ukrainian Prisoners of War (POWs) in 2024, and in 2025 according to the UN, the situation has only gotten worse. An entire system is dedicated to breaking down every trace of humanity in an individual through extreme pain, deprivation of basic necessities, and relentless humiliation. This system operates with the involvement of prison supervisors and close coordination between the Russian Federal Security Service and the Federal Penitentiary Service. The prison service has a long record of employing various forms of torture, with cases documented even before Russia's full-scale invasion of Ukraine. Now, faced with an enemy they despise and granted absolute power over prisoners of war, there are no limits to their creativity in cruelty.

Do we really need to know the details? A haunting question.

The answer is a resolute yes, we do.

And why?

To honour those, who had the courage to report and resist their oppressive treatment. It is about restoring dignity—even after death—to those who did not survive and came home as mutilated bodies, or never returned at all. And it is about prevention, raising our voices among the many who demand that the Red Cross and other neutral organisations be granted access to the sites where prisoners are held. In 2025, the Russian Federation adopted a law removing prison staff from accountability for the torture of detainees. The situation is now even worse than before—torture has been given official justification. In reality, the cruelty inflicted far surpasses anything one might witness in a film. Yet, the testimonies of survivors also offer hope, showing that courage and determination can bring people back even from the darkest depths of despair.

Many of our stories concern prisoners from the elite Azov Regiment, subject of a campaign of misinformation and vilification from the Russians as 'Nazis', so we have started with a short description of that regiment.

The Azov Regiment

We wanted to provide some context about the Azov Regiment. Among others, they were the main defenders of Mariupol for 86 days out of which 82 were under full siege (from 24 February to 20 May 2022). After the Russian invasion suddenly began in February 2022 they stood up and defended their land from Russian aggression. It was Russia that crossed the border of a neighbouring country under false pretences. Mariupol, a prosperous Ukrainian city before the invasion, suffered unbelievable destruction. It was Russia that killed 100,000 civilians in the city. It was Russia that destroyed practically every building in the city.

Russia needed a pretext to convince its own people that it was always on the side of righteousness, fighting evil, and therefore justified in actions such as bombing residential high-rises and, eventually, the Azovstal steelworks. Since the Azov regiment had been defending Ukraine since 2014—when Russia's invasion of eastern Ukraine first began, though Moscow initially denied its presence until the full-scale assault in 2022—it became crucial for Russia to discredit Azov. To this end, Russia branded the fighters as fascists deserving extermination and claimed Ukrainian territories as historically theirs. Thus, in the 21st century, we are confronted with the spectacle of one state invading another, declaring its people adherents of Nazi ideology, and using that lie to justify territorial annexation. Those who resist with weapons in hand are, by this twisted logic, condemned as the 'worst Nazis of all.'

We are happy to report that investigations in the US and the UK, as well as those of independent news agencies have found no evidence to support the claim that the Azov defenders committed human rights abuses or were neo-Nazis.

But what is Nazism, this thing that Putin allegedly started the war over. According to the Wikipedia definition Nazism is a form of fascism with disdain for liberal democracy and the parliamentary system. It incorporates a dictatorship, fervent antisemitism, anti-communism, anti-Slavism, racism, white supremacy, Nordicism, social Darwinism and the use of eugenics in its creed. But Azov is a military regiment, not a political party and Ukraine is a parliamentary republic with a multi-party system and a president. Though every country has its internal problems, we never experienced fervent antisemitic events, such as the recent one in Dagestan, Russia, when a crowd attacked the international airport in Makhachkala seeking out Jews.

Anti-communism is fundamental to our national politics now, because the people of Ukraine suffered greatly during Soviet communist rule. If you google Holodomor you will find out how many millions of Ukrainians were starved to death. We have documented mass executions of Ukrainians, and there is a special term, the Executed Renaissance, for a whole generation of Ukrainian poets, writers and artists who were executed between 1920s and 1930s. Common people whose lives were destroyed by the regime are without number. So we have the right to grieve for them, to honour their memory and to call out their executioners, even if some of them are long dead. We do not want our streets named in their honour and their monuments adorning our parks.

So, who are the real fascists in this case? From open sources we can find this definition: 'Fascism is a far-right, authoritarian, ultranationalist political ideology and movement' (Wikipedia).

Here we re-emphasise that Azov is not a political party, but rather a formation of the National Guard of Ukraine. And, as such they are supposed to love their country, however they do that on the territory of their country and it is still incredible that Ukrainians have to explain their right to love Ukraine in Ukraine. To investigate further, fascism has the following characteristics:

- Dictatorial leader
- Centralised autocracy
- Militarism
- Forcible suppression of opposition
- Belief in a natural social hierarchy
- Subordination of individual interests for the perceived good of the nation and race
- Strong regimentation of society and the economy

How many of those can be found in modern day Russia?

The two main accusations thrown at the Azov defenders are: the chevron shoulder insignia on their uniforms and the torch processions. There is also a ridiculous one about tattoos, which Russians believe to be a sign of fascism as well. So much so that a Ukrainian warrior Vasil Pelesh had his arm chopped off in 2014 when he was captured by the Russians because he had a Trident tattoo. To be clear and most readers will know, the Trident is an official emblem of Ukraine. From 2022 onwards, in so-called 'filtration' camps—established for refugees from Ukraine attempting to cross into Russian-occupied territories—people, especially men, have been forced to undress so their bodies can be inspected for tattoos.

So let's return to the chevrons, or shoulder sleeve insignia, of Azov.

When the Azov soldiers chose their symbols, they looked only to Ukrainian traditions, with no connection to medieval German or Nazi imagery. The emblem they adopted was long used by Volyn noblemen and Cossack families. Known as the 'Hook,' it represents the intersection of the letters I and N, standing for their main slogan: *Idea of the Nation*. The N follows old Ukrainian orthography, written as it appeared in early Cossack and pre-reform Russian documents before Peter the Great's spelling changes, while the I remains the same in both old and modern usage.

The wolf's hook was one of the sub-runes, originally a pagan symbol believed to protect a men from werewolves. The meaning of a wolf's hook is a trap for a wolf. It can be found nowadays on the coat of arms of many German towns e.g. Erwitte, Dassendorf, Wolfstein. In the 15th century, the Wolf's Hook was sometimes used as a symbol of peasant uprisings, and it came to represent freedom and independence. In military heraldry, it also signified power, protection of its bearer, and the mirroring back of any attack. As you see, the symbol Azov uses has a rich history.

The Azov defenders, including soldiers of the Azov Brigade, were true patriots who, against all odds, stood against the Russian invasion to defend their homeland. Yet Putin needed to present his people with 'fascists' to justify the war. It is no surprise, then, that show trials were staged in Russian towns, where Azov defenders—some of whom had not even been soldiers before the 2022 invasion—were sentenced to 20–30 years in prison simply for being labelled 'fascists.' On 16 May 2022, the President of Ukraine ordered the evacuation of everyone from the Azovstal plant, assuring that they would be exchanged within three to four months. The Russians, however, branded them prisoners of war, even though the Mariupol defenders had neither raised a white flag nor surrendered with their hands in the air. In total, 2,500 Azov defenders were taken into captivity.

At the time of writing, more than 1,000 Azov defenders remain imprisoned in Russian camps (Ukrainska Pravda, 29 May 2025). They are routinely tortured, with many losing 20–50 kilograms during captivity. By contrast, Ukraine allocates 10,000 Hryvnia per month to feed each Russian prisoner of war and provides medical care when needed. No such care is given to the Azov defenders. On 29 June 2022, the Russians carried out a terrorist attack on one of the barracks holding Azov POWs, killing an estimated 53 men—burned alive

Our mission is to ensure the world does not forget our heroes, who suffer only for defending their country from invaders. Azov is not some secretive fascist organisation—it is an official unit of the Ukrainian military, part of the National Guard, once based in Mariupol, the city Russia destroyed in 2022. Founded in 2014, Azov helped save Mariupol from the self-proclaimed Donetsk People's Republic that same year and remained there as its garrison. For anyone doubting how prosperous Mariupol once was—and what it has become—there are countless photos, videos, and survivors' testimonies. To cover up its war crimes, Russia goes so far as to blame the city's defenders for its destruction. The resistance at Azovstal steelworks was nothing less than heroic. It ended only when many fighters, including their commander Denis Prokopenko, surrendered under orders from Ukraine's high command. At the time, Kremlin spokesman Dmitry Peskov claimed President Putin had guaranteed they would be treated 'in accordance with international standards.' Instead, Ukraine's soldiers have been vilified by Russian propaganda as 'neo-Nazis' and now endure abuse and torture in captivity.

FREE THE AZOV DEFENDERS! That is our message to the world.

What happened at Olenivka

'Probably the smell is what I remember most. The incomprehensible, poisonous smell of smoke… burnt bodies.' This is how the 23-year-old Azov soldier 'Craft' recalled the night of 29 July 2022 in an interview with Olena Barsukova for the newspaper Ukrainska Pravda exactly two years later.

Olenivka was a small rural settlement of some 4000 inhabitants at the time of the census in 2001, and almost all Ukrainian speakers. Only 20 kilometres from Donetsk city, in 2014 it came under the control of the separatist Donetsk Peoples Republic and after the 2022 full scale invasion the Russians established a prison camp in a nearby village for which this little Ukrainian town is now notorious. Look it up online and you will find it synonymous with the Olenivka prison massacre of 29 July 2022, one of the most horrific war crimes in a conflict where such crimes have become commonplace. At Olenivka, 193 Azov prisoners were deliberately transferred to 'Barrack 200,' where 53 were killed in the explosion and many more were seriously wounded.

The Times on 31 July 2022 hardly noticed the event, burying it in a longer article about grain exports and obscuring the truth by giving prominence to Russian misinformation propaganda:

'Moscow and Kyiv continued to trade accusations over an explosion early on Friday at a prison camp in Olenivka, in Russian-occupied Ukraine, in which at least 50 captured Ukrainian soldiers died and many dozens were injured. Both sides have blamed each other.

The Russian defence ministry claimed Ukrainian forces had used powerful American-made High Mobility Artillery Rocket System (HIMARS) rockets to attack the camp in what it claimed was a warning by Kyiv to their own forces of their possible fate if they surrendered. US officials said they had found no evidence to back such claims, while Ukraine accused Russia of conducting the attack to cover up the 'torture and shooting' of Ukrainian prisoners held there.'

The Guardian's Luke Harding four days later published a more graphic account making it clear that Ukrainian 'intelligence, satellite data and phone intercepts' showed that it was a 'callous and premeditated [Russian] war crime'.

The 2024 *Ukrainska Pravda* interview provides an account of what really happened on that night by a witness who survived.

*   *   *

Twenty-three-year-old soldier 'Craft' (his call sign, chosen for his love of Minecraft) had been a student of cybersecurity, telecommunications, and radio engineering. As the situation in Ukraine grew tense, he transferred to the military faculty in 2020 and soon after decided to join the Azov Regiment.

When the Russian attack on Ukraine started on 22 February 2022 Craft was in Mariupol and defended the city together with his brothers-in-arms. In April that year he was at the Azovstal works first as a group commander, then as a divisional commander. After being wounded, he remained at the command post to manage the fighting from there. On the night of 14-15 May, the Azov commander informed them that, in order to save the wounded, the regiment would have to enter Russian captivity, under an agreement that they would be exchanged and sent home within three or four months. On 20 May, Craft and his brothers-in-arms were taken to the Olenivka camp, where they were searched and placed in barracks designed for 50 but forced to hold 300 POWs.

He was glad his sleeping bag and mat had not been confiscated as he had to sleep on the ground. Food was scarce as the kitchen was not ready to feed so many captives. All the POWs were tortured although he personally escaped the worst treatment as a senior soldier. He was told to denounce his commander for a fake offense in return for early exchange. This he refused to do.

Several days before the terrorist act the Russians took 50-60 people from three barracks where the Azov defenders had been kept and moved them to Barrack 200, which was converted from a former camp shop. The camp governor told them that they were being moved because their barracks was going to be repaired but the prisoners did not believe him as that explanation was illogical. If the authorities really wanted to repair their former barracks they would have moved one barrack, repaired it and moved the captives back. You did not need lists and people from three different barracks. There seemed to be no logic in their choice of prisoners: there were commanders, soldiers, artillerymen, intelligence officers and even those who were civilians before joining the Azov units on 24 February. The only thing they had in common was that they had all been Azov soldiers.

The POW working group at Barrack 200 later confirmed that that particular barrack had been specially prepared for them.

After preparing the barrack the guards moved their observation point 30-50 meters away from the barrack fence and fortified it by digging trenches around it. And on the day of the tragedy ten unknown people in black balaclavas without any identification signs came to guard Barrack 200. Before that it was guarded by the camp warders with the insignia of the 'Federal Penitentiary Service' on their clothes.

The day before the terrorist act the Russians surrounded the fence around Barrack 200 with barbed wire.

Living conditions in Barrack 200 were very bad as there was very little space for all the POWs who had been moved there. They were sleeping practically on top of each other. It was summer and scorching hot but there was nowhere even to wash your face. There were two 1000 litre barrels of water but they didn't have taps.

It is also interesting that on the day of the explosion electricians came to the barrack to connect the lights. All the Barrack 200 inmates had been taken outside while this was happening, so they did not know what the Russians were doing in the barrack at that time.

The explosion happened just before lights out that same day.

The day before, on 28 July, Craft was walking through the exercise area after dinner and noticed a drone hovering over the barrack. At the time he didn't know enough about drones to identify it but later found out that it was a DJI Matrice because he had noticed its characteristic red-green lights. They are visible when the operator forgets to switch on stealth mode. He pointed them out to his brothers-in-arms and they all lifted their heads to look at the drone. The pilot must have then realised, and quickly switched off the lights. At that moment the Grad multiple rocket launcher system started firing from inside the camp walls. This was nothing new as the Russians had done this many times before.

That evening all the Barrack 200 inmates were forbidden to go outside the sleeping area of the barrack, except for going to the toilet, but were limited to going one at a time.

Craft went to sleep and woke up from the deafening sound of an explosion and an intense pain in his stomach. He felt that something was wrong; looking down he found a hole in his stomach, with internal abdominal bleeding, and his whole body felt as if it was burning on the inside. He examined himself and found his limbs were intact. Then he saw heavy smoke inside the barrack and understood he had to get out. The interior was in flames, and he saw the burnt bodies of his brothers-in-arms. They were practically melted into their beds. His friends 'Tower' and 'August' were dead.

He told the interviewer 'Perhaps what I remember most of all is the smell. The incomprehensible, poisonous smell of smoke, burnt bodies, blazing fire over the roof and glass wool that is coming down on me like thousands of tiny needles'. At some point he found himself in a sort of noise isolation when everything around him went in slow motion as if he was watching from the side. This went on until he was carried out and put on the tarmac. Craft called to one of his brothers-in-arms who was running past, and he examined him. At that moment the Russians started to fire into the air. The injured POWs were not allowed to go outside the kerbs. They were ordered to lie on the tarmac and not on the grass, where they remained for about an hour before they were examined by the doctors. After what Craft said felt like forever, the POW doctors were allowed to treat the wounded and assist those who could still be saved.

The POW medics had only minimal supplies of medicine and the guards just threw them a bunch of sheets for the wounded to be bandaged. When Craft asked for painkillers, the answer was that there were only cold powders with paracetamol in them. He refused as he thought that it would not help with his type of injuries. The guards actually did nothing to help, they did not try to put out the fire in the barrack, and they did not help evacuate and transport the wounded before dawn. It would have still been possible to save some of the injured but they were just left to bleed to death without any help from the guards.

Craft was in the second priority group for evacuation. 'Lemko', his brother -in-arms, was sitting next to him, bending over him and talking, trying not to let him fall asleep. Somewhere around 6 o'clock in the morning, when it was light outside, Craft was loaded onto a Ural truck, and the injured men were piled up and taken to hospital. Craft's diagnosis was a penetrating wound to the abdomen, an impacted pelvic bone, shrapnel in the right hip joint, multiple burns and small shrapnel wounds all over his body. He learned from the surgeons who operated on him that at the time of his arrival he had a little more than a litre of blood left in his body. They said that he was lucky his heart kept pumping. They believed it was because he was a sportsman, and his body was in good physical shape.

They received meals three times a day on weekdays at the hospital. On weekends, however, the food was worse, as the hospital managers went home and the women in the kitchen stole food to take to their families.

The doctors generally treated them well, providing professional medical care, and there were enough painkillers available. Their guards were young men from the guard battalion, who behaved like ordinary people. They were curious about Mariupol and eager to hear information first-hand. Of course, they had been indoctrinated and asked questions about 'biolaboratories.'

But some of the cleaning women talked about Bandera, Nazis and fascists. One of them even said 'You killed my son, why should I clean your room?'.

'Then don't clean it.' Craft answered.

Russian journalists visited the hospital to make video reports. Craft did not remember the first one as it was made when he was still unconscious in the intensive care unit.

The injured prisoners were told that it was Ukraine that fired at their barrack with HIMARS. At that time they did not even know what a HIMARS was. Craft saw HIMARS in action for the first time when one of the guards showed him a video of a HIMARS rocket destroying a column of military equipment. After viewing the video he pointed out that if it had been HIMARS, nothing would have been left of them or their barrack.

It was as clear as day to the prisoners that it was a Russian act. The prisoners were all gathered in one particular barrack and the Russians fired a Grad missile from inside the camp. It was a clear provocation. Craft believed that a thermobaric charge was placed inside the barrack by the 'electricians' and that the charge was detonated during the night. It was a planned terrorist attack.

Once a low life journalist from the DNR Russian YouTube channel came to interview Craft. He showed him some of his interviews with the old women from the trauma department of the same hospital. One of them showed him her arm which was presumably shot by a sniper. The journalist wanted him to comment on that. He told the journalist that he condemned any illegal action against civilians. The journalist did not like Craft's comment and angrily left the ward.

In the hospital Craft was in a ward on the top floor where the security battalion headquarters were located. A soldier, one of the guards entered his ward and asked, 'Are you willing to rattle around for 12 hours a Ural truck?'.

At that time he was just starting to walk after the injury but he replied jokingly 'If it's for an exchange, I would be willing to rattle for a day in a Ural. But if it's just for transportation to another place in Russia, then certainly not.' The guard then told Craft that there was going to be an exchange and put his name on the exchange list.

Craft was soon on his way. Packed like sardines in Ural trucks and then flown via Moscow to Gomel the prisoners thought they were being transported to another colony in Russia. They thought that perhaps the Russians needed a few statements from them at a show trial. But at Gomel the Belarusians entered the buses and said 'Guys, calm down, don't worry. You are going to be exchanged.'

When they reached Ukraine someone said 'Guys, you are home.' They saw a lot of other Ukrainian soldiers at the exchange. Everyone had changed a lot after being in Russian captivity. Craft himself lost 27kg while some others lost 40-50 kg—they were shadows of their previous selves.

Craft rejoined the army as soon as he was physically able, first in a radio unit but soon back with the Azov regiment. Captivity had changed him and although his memory has deteriorated and he will never be as physically fit as before, he told the interviewer 'I have become better for the profession because I have no emotion at all. I always make decisions with a cool head.'

His final words at the interview were

'My comrades must be exchanged, because the terrorist attack in Olenivka is neither the first nor the last act of intimidation—a demonstration of Russia's impunity. I spent four months in captivity, and some have been held there for three years. We must fight for them. We need a victory, not 'peaceful' arguments.'

Based on an interview with 'Craft' by Elena Barsukova in Ukrainska Pravda 29 July 2024 (https://life.pravda.com.ua/society/azovec-kraft-rozpoviv-pro-terakt-v-olenivci-ta-yak-vizhiv-pislya-vibuhu-302875/)

Olexander Zarva, a Border Guard in Russian Captivity

Olexander Zarva was a border guard in Luhansk until his capture by the Russians in April 2022. He was freed in January 2024 as part of that year's largest prisoner exchange. This is his story.

After studying at university Olexander began work as a foundryman in the injection moulding section at the large Novator factory in the central Ukrainian city of Khmelnitsky. He has always been very patriotic and since he was a student in his teens had a tattoo of the Ukrainian Trident on his arm. So in 2015, as the war in the east of Ukraine was taking off, he volunteered at the military recruitment office and was sent to serve as a border guard in Luhansk, defending Ukraine's eastern border against Russian incursion. He was in the 3rd Yevhen Pikysov Luhansk Border Detachment, named after a Hero of Ukraine. By 2022 he was a senior sergeant and worked as an Armoured Personnel Carrier (APC) driver.

On 15th of January 2022 Olexander was sent on a mission to Valuyki, a hamlet near the Russian border of the Luhansk region. On the night of the 23rd February 2022 Russian helicopters crossed the Ukrainian border and the full-scale invasion started. Olexander's detachment was spread all along the border and although the border guards were well trained there were not enough personnel and military equipment to resist the enemy. The border guards had to retreat west in the direction of Kharkiv, to the town of Borova. In early April they were defending Borova and had destroyed a column of Russian forces before they were surrounded by the enemy. The border guards were given orders to break out of the encirclement but at that point unfortunately they were unable to do that.

Olexander destroyed his APC to prevent it from falling into enemy hands. He and the other soldiers then got into their patrol car and tried to break through, but the Russians opened fire on their vehicle. One border guard was killed, while Olexander and another were wounded. As Olexander was providing first aid to his comrade, they were captured. This happened on April 13, 2022, and for a long time Olexander was considered missing.

Still in shock and wounded, Olexander and his fellow guard had their hands tied by their captors and they were blindfolded and taken from place to place. Eventually Olexander realised that they had crossed the border into Russia. At first they were placed in a tented POW camp, where they were interrogated. The Russians wanted to know who they were, where they were from and where they served. Their captors were real vandals and marauders, taking away all the prisoners' personal belongings, even the golden cross on a golden chain that was given to Olexander when he was baptised. Olexander said that if he had had gold teeth he was sure the Russians would have pulled them out.

The wounded border guards were given limited 'medical help'. Olexander had a shrapnel wound in his leg so the doctors operated but without any anaesthesia.

They made a cut in his leg, cleaned the wound and then sewed it up. That was it. He stayed in that camp until the 25th of April. It was Easter and on the second day of Easter the imprisoned border guards were transported to a pre-trial detention centre.

It was there that all the horror started: beatings, torture, bullying, abuse, insults and humiliation. Sometimes their gaolers sprayed gas into the cells. Some POWs went mad. Olexander had never before seen such atrocities against human beings. He could not understand what harm they had ever done to their torturers, who claimed to be Slavic people—supposedly brothers, who were meant to be friendly towards one another. Olexander could not imagine what Ukrainians had done to deserve such inhumanity. The captors set dogs on the POWs, poured boiling water on their tattoos or cut them out with a saw, and beat them mercilessly—the torture was unbearable. His own tattoo, depicting the Ukrainian Trident and the folk hero Kotyhoroshko, became a constant target, with the guards insisting he remove it.

Kotyhoroshko is the hero of a well-known Ukrainian folk tale. He was a boy of extraordinary strength born from a pea, who overcomes challenges with courage and wit to defeat an evil sorcerer and rescue his family. He represents resilience and the triumph of good over evil in Ukrainian folklore.

'They gave me a brick to scrape off the tattoo but I said I wouldn't do it. They beat me, bullied me, but I didn't allow myself to do it,' said Olexander in a later interview.

The food they were given was worse than what one would feed an animal: boiled potato peels, served so hot that the captives could not eat them quickly. If they failed to finish their meal within five minutes, their torturers dragged them out of their cells and beat them. As a result, the POWs survived mostly on small pieces of bread and water. The imprisoned border guards remained there until October 1st, when they were transported to another prison in Kineshma, in Russia's Ivanovo region.

Kineshma was where they were to serve their sentence—without any trial. As a 'welcome,' they were mercilessly beaten upon arrival. From then on, a strict routine followed: at 6 a.m. they had to get up and sing the Russian anthem, then came breakfast.

There were six men in their cell. Breakfast was porridge, served in only three plates, so two people had to share each plate—about three or four spoonfuls per person. At first, they were given bread with the porridge, but soon their captors decided even that was 'too much' and stopped providing bread.

Lunch was the same: three plates for the cell, filled with thin prison soup, five spoonfuls each. For the main course, there were only two plates of some unidentifiable food, meaning three men had to share one plate. Dinner followed the same pattern, without bread. In the beginning, they sometimes received tea or a jelly-like drink, but that too was eventually taken away.

There was water from the tap, but it was undrinkable. Under such conditions, many prisoners lost their teeth. When Olexander was first captured, he weighed 115 kg. Within several months he had lost 45 kg, his weight dropping to just 70.

The prisoners were not allowed to sit or lie down during the day, forced instead to stand for sixteen hours, even while eating their meals. They had to ask permission to open or close the window or to use the toilet. After lights out they could lie down, but often they were woken in the middle of the night, taken from their cells only to be beaten, and then returned.

They had to do their own laundry in the cell, using washing powder in icy cold water. The Russians never changed the sheets. Once a week the prisoners were taken to a bathhouse, where they could also shave. They had to mend their own clothes, and heating was switched on or off at the whim of the warders. At first they were forced to walk in slippers, later they were issued boots. Time outside was limited to short walks in the prison yard, and only during summer.

As for 'culture' they were made to read the works of Lenin and Stalin. The Russians were educating them, trying to make them Russian patriots. Then the warders brought them a list of 'Heroes of Russia'—soldiers who had been killed in battles in the Luhansk region and near Kharkiv. The POWs had to learn the list by heart: names, surnames, patronymics, dates of birth and death, everything. After some time their jailors would come to check how well the prisoners had memorised the list. Any mistake and the prisoner would be beaten. Olexander did not have a single unbroken rib on both sides of his body. Their warders would switch on Russian songs on the loudspeaker and make the prisoners sing them. Their jailers would then tell them that the whole of Ukraine had already been conquered by Russia. But the POWs did not believe it. They had discovered from those lists of 'heroes', the dates and places of death. And it showed that the Russian forces were at the same positions all the time. They had not been able to advance anywhere, let alone over all Ukraine.

The prisoners were also made to shout slogans against the Ukrainian president. The Russians had whole lists of anti-Ukrainian slogans. Olexander refused to shout such slogans as they were ridiculously wrong. Olexander's warders ordered him to write a statement to the effect that he, Olexander Zarva, asked to be executed as he refused to obey orders. Then the date and Olexander's signature. Twice Olexander was taken to be executed but he was not shot. Olexander did not want to state anything so completely untrue.

Interrogations were conducted regularly. The Russians wanted to know where the Ukrainian bases were and other important military information. As Olexander had been a driver, after several interrogations, the Russians lost interest in him.

The most difficult thing in captivity was waiting for the exchange. And it was very important to support their comrades. Some POWs made loops from their sheets to hang themselves. Olexander did his best to stop them saying that it would be a great blow and tragedy for their parents and loved ones. And the Russians would not return their bodies to Ukraine. They would sooner put them into a hole and cover them with earth somewhere under the prison fence. Patience and more patience was essential. Many of the prisoners would pray as they believed that only God could help them. They also continued to talk among themselves in their cell and although they were not allowed to speak Ukrainian they would do so at risk of punishment.

The main task for the Russian warders was to write reports about war crimes committed by the POWs. There were regular visits by prosecutors from the occupied territories who handed out sentences to prisoners accused of such crimes. One prisoner got 15 years and another got 25 years. They were taken away, nobody knows where and never seen again.

Olexander tried to explain to one of his interrogators that he was a border guard and his task had been to watch the border of his country, to protect that border from intruders. What kind of crime did he commit by guarding the border of his country? But his reasoning did not hit home. The interrogators would bring up arguments like 'it's your government that is to blame', 'it's Zelensky who is to blame', 'they don't want to exchange you', and so on and so forth. And one of the interrogators said, 'If we hadn't attacked you, we know for a fact that your Zelensky wanted to capture Archangelsk and Kuban.' In fact, those Russians were completely uneducated people. For example, when the warders tried to solve crosswords or played a game called 'Cities' the POWs could hear them say 'A city starting with the letter A?' and the answer would be 'Australia'. The POWs would just laugh at their ignorance.

The warders' uniforms were marked 'Spetsnaz' (Russian Special Forces) though they were wearing Ukrainian army boots and some pieces of Ukrainian uniform which they had taken from Ukrainian prisoners. The prisoners were forbidden to look their captors in the eye; they had to walk bent over, with their hands kept behind their back. There was one young Ukrainian soldier, a fan of the Ultras (patriotic football fans), whom the Russians called Bandera after the Second World War Ukrainian nationalist who fought the Soviets. He and Olexander were the star attractions of the Russian 'programme' of torture. The Russians enjoyed torturing them because of their tattoos and set their dogs on Olexander and his friend.

One day the Russians gave Olexander a piece of paper dictating that he should write, 'Dear Mum. Everything is OK with me. I am well. I am alive and I am healthy.' His mother received the letter and wrote back to Olexander but the warders did not give him her reply. However Olexander had been reported missing for half a year and it was due to his letter that she found out he was a POW.

Some Russian volunteers occasionally visited the prison and allowed certain POWs to make video calls to their families. But not everyone had that privilege— Olexander among them. Russian lawyers also came, asking the POWs if everything was 'all right.' The answer was always yes, for they knew that any complaint would mean a beating as soon as the visitors left. The beatings finally stopped only when the authorities began preparing prisoners for exchange.

One evening, just after dinner, the door to their cell opened and they heard the order: *'Prisoner of war Zarva Olexander, pack up and leave.'* At first, Olexander thought he was simply being moved to another cell. Along with three other prisoners, he was taken to the main building and ordered to change into a Ukrainian uniform. Only then did they realize they were to be exchanged.

When they left the prison, the temperature outside was minus 28 degrees Celsius. Dressed only in their uniforms, with no heating in the police van, they endured a four-hour drive. The cold was so intense that their tooth enamel began to peel away. When the van finally stopped, the Russians put sacks over their heads and transferred them to a bus bound for the border.

When Olexander left the bus he saw Ukrainian soldiers. His first words were 'Friends, please give me a cigarette.' Then they started singing the anthem of Ukraine. After that Olexander was given a mobile phone and called his friend because he had completely forgotten his mother's phone number. His friend ran to his mother's home to tell her the good news. When Olexander was able to speak to her she could not stop crying. She could hardly believe that her son was finally back from Russian captivity. It was so emotional for Olexander to hear his mother's voice. Unfortunately, his father did not live to see his son back—he had died during Olexander's captivity.

For some time Olexander could hardly believe that he was not in the camp and nobody would shout, 'Get up, you sons of bitches, etc, etc, etc.' but with time when his mother and his friends began coming to see him Olexander gradually came to realise that he really was back from Russian captivity. He still had to take sleeping pills. The other POWs were in a much worse state. At first Olexander was treated in hospital. 'Wonderful food', he told an interviewer adding that they feed the released POWs like prize turkeys. And such a kind and humane attitude.

Olexander will have to spend some more time in rehabilitation and then he is planning to go back to the front and fight. He believes that good will triumph. He said that the Ukrainians are not to blame in this war. To this day it's hard for Olexander to understand the true reasons why Russia started the war but he knows we must all fight back. We must all stand to the last. We are unbreakable. Our people are unconquerable and enduring. Our war is the people's war. Ukraine will prevail!

Source: Based on an interview with Suspilne News, Khmelnitsky, January and February 2024 (YouTube https://www.youtube.com/watch?v=HhLVZHk0SAw, and articles https://suspilne.media/khmelnytskiy)

Paramedics in captivity: Tayra and her Angels

Not only Ukrainian military personnel are taken into captivity by the Russian forces. Prisoners include private citizens—paramedics like Yulia Paievska and Volodymyr Tatarenko.

Volodymyr Tatarenko was born in Mariupol and had an advertising business in the city with his father. When Russia attacked the Donbas in 2014 he became an active member of a voluntary medical organisation known as Tayra's Angels, named after its leader the legendary paramedic Yulia Paevska whose call sign was Tayra. Volodymyr played a key role and helped treat and evacuate many wounded soldiers from the battlefield.

Who was Tayra?
Yulia Paevska was born in 1968 and brought up in Kyiv by her grandfather, a veteran of the Siege of Leningrad. A ceramicist and designer by profession her first medical experience came from awareness of sports injuries through her interest in aikido. She was an accomplished aikido fighter and coach, president of the Ukrainian Aikido Federation.

In 2013 she became a volunteer paramedic during the Euromaidan protests in Kyiv and when war broke out in the Donbas in 2014 she volunteered as a paramedic, adopting the call sign 'Tayra'. She trained about 8000 volunteer paramedics in tactical medicine and liaised between civilians and the army in frontline areas—supporting many without medical coverage. Soon she had set up the ambulance service for military and civilian victims of the war that became known as 'Tayra's Angels'. It was a voluntary organisation, mainly funded by small donations from individuals, but, as she told Ukrainska Pravda in 2018 'I don't like the word 'volunteer'. It has a touch of unprofessionalism. In four years, we are already such pros … We are volunteers—those who consciously and sincerely do what we do'. They saved some 500 lives.

When the full scale invasion began in 2022 she spent the first three weeks working in the Mariupol hospital helping to triage the wounded as they arrived. There were a large number of women and infants living in the hospital basement because the hospital had an electricity generator and a reliable water supply. These women were desperate to get out of Mariupol into Zaporizhzhia, which was in Ukrainian territory, and there were rumours that others had managed to get out through the so-called safe corridor. Tayra knew that there was a bus they could use and decided to take the risk of driving the women and their babies out. She thought that no one would harm women and children.

On 15 March, the day before their journey began, Tayra gave Associated Press journalists her photographs and films documenting the siege of Mariupol during the first three weeks of the full-scale invasion. The material, captured on her body camera while she and the Angels worked in the city, was intended to show the world the horrors that had befallen Mariupol.

On 16 March, as they drove the bus out of Mariupol, Tayra and the driver were detained by Russian soldiers and taken into captivity. The women and children were released.

This marked the beginning of her three months of imprisonment.

Shortly after her release, in an interview with Deutsche Welle journalist Tamara Kiptenko, Tayra was asked how she had endured the physical and mental hardships of Russian captivity. She spoke stoically about the physical conditions, mentioning only that her first prison was in Donetsk, where she was held alongside women from the National Guard, Azov, and other military units, as well as civilians. Twenty-two women were crammed into a cell measuring just 3 by 6 meters, with only 10 bunks to share.

They were not allowed to sit during the day. One of the women in that cell was 7 months pregnant.

Food was scarce—'just enough to keep us alive'—and by the second week there was no soap. Throughout her captivity, she had only the clothes she was wearing when she was arrested. She was denied medical care and any contact by phone. Describing those early weeks more vividly, she said: 'the days merged into each other—no sleep, no food, almost no water...'

Tayra told the journalist that she had been physically strong before her imprisonment, thanks not only to years of martial arts and yoga but also to her recent training for the Invictus Games. She had been invited to compete in May 2022, but captivity made that impossible. Instead, her daughter took her place, and won a bronze medal in archery. The publicity around her absence ensured the world learned what had happened to her.

Psychologically, she remained resilient: 'I did not collapse, I kept my dignity, I knew I had done nothing wrong.' But the pressure was relentless. Some of her early cellmates in Donetsk were less able to withstand it, suffering terribly from not knowing the fate of their families.

Her own situation was different. The authorities were searching for Ukrainian agents in Mariupol—'on the territory of the Donetsk People's Republic'—and she was told to expect a death sentence as a collaborator with a foreign power, Ukraine. Guards taunted her with lines such as: 'You will die, so you might as well kill yourself.' As she later observed, 'that would have been very convenient for them.'

Her captors knew about the video material she had released to the international press. They bombarded her with lies and misinformation—not only about herself but also about the course of the war. Still, she remained steadfast, convinced that 'you can't believe the enemy—they either distort facts or tell straightforward lies.' The few fragments of reliable news she managed to gather—Russia's lack of progress and its retreat from Kyiv—only strengthened her faith in Ukraine.

The Russians went so far as to make a propaganda documentary about her. She did not trust the affable television crew and was acutely aware she had to choose her words carefully, hoping to make it difficult for them to distort the truth in the editing room. In the end, however, they twisted her statements into what she called an 'absurdity,' portraying her as a 'Nazi,' a 'murderer,' and even a spy.

Her message to other prisoners is clear: never believe what the Russians tell you, especially their claims that the world has abandoned you or that Ukraine is finished. Like her, you must trust that the torture and psychological pressure will one day come to an end.

For Tayra, that trust was finally rewarded when she was included in a prisoner exchange on 17 June 2022. Since her release, Tayra has devoted herself to initiatives addressing the issue of captivity. She has testified before the US Congress and co-founded the Ukrainian charity 'Mechta' (The Dream), which supports the families of prisoners as well as those of fallen and missing soldiers and civilians.

In 2023 she fulfilled her long-delayed goal of competing in the Invictus Games, where she won a silver medal in swimming and a bronze medal in archery. That same year, her courage and resilience were recognized internationally when she received the US International Women of Courage Award.

Volodymyr Tatarenko, a medic from Mariupol

This is the story of one of Tayra's 'Angels', Volodymyr Tatarenko. Volodymyr had been volunteering with Tayra's Angels since 2014. When Russia invaded Ukraine on 24th of February 2022 he and his family were in Mariupol. Volodymyr decided to join the regular army as there was a military unit stationed in his neighbourhood. However on the day he went to sign up there were very long lines of volunteers (at least 150) and the recruiters did not seem to know what to do with all the volunteers.

At the same time the unit was being shelled by Russian aviation so Volodymyr called the Angels. They went to Hospital 555, an emergency hospital, where Tayra gave them a car to transport the wounded and explained what they had to do. Their main task was to defend and protect the hospital. Volodymyr and 10 others from the territorial defence unit did their best to help the hospital operate in conditions of war. It was real hell there, full of wounded soldiers and large numbers of civilians all needing medical help, including many children, women and the elderly. There were horrific scenes.

When a missile struck Orbita, a computer equipment repair center in Mariupol, they rescued a young girl, about 10 or 12 years old, from a damaged car nearby. As they pulled her out, a shell fragment fell, and the child's mother picked it up, convinced it was something from her daughter's body—an internal organ. 'Look,' she cried. 'It's something that fell out of my daughter!'

On another occasion, parents brought in their baby. All three—the mother, father, and infant—were wounded and needed treatment. After the operation, they stayed in the emergency hospital's bomb shelter. The baby required nappies, bottles, formula, and teats, so the task was to search the ruined city for these essentials. Despite their efforts, the child did not survive.

All the while, battles raged in the city and the Russian encirclement grew ever tighter. It soon became clear that the hospital would have to be evacuated. The operating theatres, located on the upper floors, had to be moved underground because of the relentless bombardment. On one occasion, while surgeons were operating on a young man, a bomb struck the building. He was buried beneath the ruins while still on the operating table. They dug his body out of the wreckage, and Volodymyr was given the grim task of taking him to the burial site.

After that, Volodymyr was assigned to the Azovstal hospital. He and the two other men in his team would rise at four or four-thirty in the morning, while it was still dark. Under cover of night, when it was harder for drones to detect them, they would go out in search of food for the hospital's 200 to 350 wounded patients.

Their next task was hospital admissions. They had to bring in newly wounded soldiers, and since the bomb shelter was underground, it was difficult to carry them down the stairs on stretchers. The work was relentless. After nearly every outing the car came back damaged. Often with a flat tire that Volodymyr would then repair.

Then a missile struck near the hospital. It was a thermobaric bomb, producing a devastating shockwave and searing gases that left soldiers with severe burns. At that moment, an operation was underway. Volodymyr's friend sent him prayers, and he read them as everyone else prayed too. In Azovstal, prayer was constant: when heading out on a mission, fixing a wheel, or simply driving, the sound of missiles or aircraft often meant there was no time to reach shelter. You understood you might not make it back.

You would try to hide under some barrels or some bits of metal and yes, at moments like that everyone would pray. Each day that you lived through in Azovstal was like going through a new stage of your life.

One of the things that affected Volodymyr most deeply was the loss of men who were killed in action or died of their wounds. In military terms, the dead were referred to as 'the 200th'. They had to take the bodies somewhere to bury them. Volodymyr found a cold dry place without sunshine and water and set up a kind of mini morgue there. The bodies of the dead were brought there and an 'Angel' would make the sign of the cross over them. Volodymyr felt hatred for the enemy and a great desire to take revenge. Everyone understood that they would never come out of Azovstal. They wanted to fight to the end as it was better for them to die honourably.

Volodymyr had a lot of tasks and responsibilities at the Zhelezyaka Hospital at the Azovstal factory and his team of three were the last to leave the hospital when they all went into Russian captivity. Before they left they had to take out the wounded and dead. Volodymyr, a native of Mariupol, acted as a guide and was the first to come out leading a group of soldiers to the place of surrender outside Azovstal.

When they were taken into captivity, their barracks at Olenivka were two-story buildings with bare rooms, lacking beds or mattresses. At first, the prisoners slept on the concrete floor; later, they were given wooden pallets.

All endured torture and beatings. After a month in captivity, a soldier was no longer the same—reduced to an empty stare, hands forced to remain behind his back. The Russians did everything they could to break them.

Volodymyr remained in Olenivka from 20 May until 3 October 2022—about four months.

Things became even worse when Volodymyr was transferred from Olenivka to Kamyshin in Russia's Volgograd region. The ordeal began with what they called the 'reception procedure': five hours of continuous beatings. It started the moment the prisoners were taken out of the vehicles—hands tied, blindfolded, forced to squat—while guards struck them with sticks and administered electric shocks.

Anyone with tattoos was singled out for even harsher punishment. One man had a scarab, another a tattoo of his pit bull. The Russians saw these as 'Nazi symbols,' branding the men as Nazis and treating them as the worst of enemies. Later, Volodymyr learned that this particular 'reception procedure' had been reported in the media as the cruellest in all of Russia. Many did not survive. Volodymyr himself fainted five times.

Amid the screams and moans of the tortured, he remembers hearing women's laughter in the background—a terrible, jarring dissonance. It was horrific.

At first, Volodymyr was held in a cell with 16 prisoners. Four were later removed, leaving twelve. They were a mixed group: a soldier, a civilian, even an elderly man who had ended up there by accident. But inside that Russian hell, it made no difference who you were. Old or young, limping from a wound, or with a broken hand left hanging useless—none of it mattered. Everyone was beaten.

The guards took particular pleasure in striking a prisoner at his weakest point, targeting old injuries again and again. Every other day, the cell was searched. Each time, the men were dragged into the corridor for another round of beatings. By then, the Russians knew each prisoner's vulnerabilities, where to hit to inflict the most pain. They especially favored the ribs. With broken ribs it was almost impossible to sleep, to turn, even to breathe properly. Prisoners were left hunched over in agony—and just as they began to recover a little, the cycle of beatings would start all over again.

There was a torture room next to Volodymyr's cell and they heard the cries of tortured people every day. Those screams were not like human screams. They were animal screams when a man was half a step away from his death. This was cruelty without any motivation at all.

The youngest prisoner in the cell was only 21, just a little older than Volodymyr's daughter. The Russians tied wires around the young man's genitals and tortured him with electric current for an hour. When he was brought back, Volodymyr asked:

'What did the Russians want to know? What kind of information were they trying to get from you?' The boy answered simply: 'Nothing.' And indeed, what could he have known? He was just a conscript—a young man, barely more than a child. To inflict such cruelty on him was horrific.

On 27 October, Volodymyr's birthday, the abuse took on a darker turn. The day before, he was taken out for interrogation. A bag was pulled over his head, wires were fastened to his little fingers, and for an hour he was tortured with electric shocks. At times his organs seemed to stop functioning altogether. The following day he still felt pain deep inside and knew something had been damaged. His interrogators believed he was a marine and therefore would not break. As they tortured him, they sneered: 'It's your birthday tomorrow, isn't it? Wouldn't it be nice to execute you then? On your gravestone the date of your death would match your birthday—47 years old!'

True to their word, they came for him at 5 a.m. the next morning. As he was taken from the barracks, the guards handed him the clothes he had been captured in, replacing his prison uniform.

It was only when he was handed a packed lunch that Volodymyr realized he was going to be exchanged. They would never give food to someone they planned to execute.

In Kamyshin prison, he often went to sleep repeating to himself: 'What doesn't kill me makes me stronger. I survived today, and that has made me a little stronger.'

The feelings that overwhelmed him during the exchange are difficult to describe. Above all, he thought: they had endured, and this was their victory.

Volodymyr and the other men who had been at the Zhelezyaka Hospital in Azovstal, and who later endured torture and suffering in Olenivka and other Russian camps, had shared everything they had—a piece of bread, a glass of water. Speaking to his interviewer, Volodymyr said that the defence of Mariupol will forever be part of the history of the war. He had seen what the Russians were capable of, and he understood the difference: Ukrainians are free people, unlike the Russians. And freedom is not something given—it is something fought for.

Supplementary information from other Azovstal medics
The surgeons at the Zhelezyaka Hospital in Azovstal operated practically non-stop. They did not take off their surgical gowns because there was a constant flow of wounded soldiers brought to the hospital. At first there were enough beds for the wounded, but later they had to put mattresses on the concrete floor or wherever they could find space and put the wounded there. As time passed and the missiles destroyed the operating theatre, the surgeons had to operate in the wards, practically in the sight of all as if it were a film. Amputation of limbs, abdominal dissection, chest dissection, everything. They had to operate in conditions that were not fit for conducting operations, since the hospital was in a bunker that could accommodate

125 people. But the fighting was intense and there were 350 wounded in the hospital. There were 4 surgeons and 3 anaesthetists. Once after a particularly fierce battle 124 wounded were brought to the hospital and they had to operate for 38 hours nonstop to save lives. The Azov defenders were truly amazing warriors. If they had light wounds they would say, 'Doctor, I don't want to waste your time. Just bandage my wound and I will go back to fight.'

On one occasion, a surgeon had just completed an operation and another wounded soldier was waiting his turn. The surgeon hesitated, guided by a sixth sense not to enter the operating room. Moments later, a thermobaric bomb struck the ventilation shafts. Powder gases poured into the bunker, and the shockwave hurled everything five to seven meters. Fire broke out and smoke filled the air, making it impossible to breathe. The operating theatre was destroyed. The surgeons managed to salvage two surgical tables and set them up in the middle of the bunker, where the operated soldiers were lying. From then on, operations had to be carried out in full view of the other wounded men. Even after the surgeons were taken into Russian captivity, they continued to care for wounded prisoners whenever possible. Around 600 injured soldiers were held in the barracks, alongside those who had not been wounded.

(From the words of Yevhen Gerashchenko, the chief surgeon of Azovstal Zhelezyaka Hospital)

The Russians beat the POWs to such an extent that broken bones in their legs would cut through the skin and stick out. A soldier with such an open fracture asked a Russian nurse to inject him with a painkiller and she answered, 'I will give you a shot but you will die before the morning.'

(From the words of 60-year-old Victor Bondarenko, one of the Azovstal paramedics)

Sources include: DW interview with Yulia Paievska 1.7.2022 ; www.dw.com/ru/tajra-o-tom-kak-byla-v-plenu-mne-skazali-chto-zhit-ne-budu/a-62333825;   RBC-Ukraine 29.10.2024 www.rbc.ua/ukr/news/vryatuvala-sotni-zhittiv-roki-viynichim-1730130756.html; Wikipedia and other sources; an interview with Volodymyr Tatarenko on the YouTube channel of 'Serdtse Azovstali' (the Heart of Azovstal) https://www.youtube.com/watch?v=3gq5_O5PM4g

Kostyantyn Bobryk, Defender of Mariupol

Kostyantyn Bobryk was born in Luhansk and lived there until 2014. In civilian life he worked as a train driver, employed by Ukrzaliznytsia (Ukrainian Railways) for more than 30 years. He had a large family—four children, one daughter and three sons.

When the war began in July 2014 and Russian forces started occupying Luhansk, Kostyantyn sent his wife and children to Mariupol, where they had relatives. He himself remained in Luhansk to continue his job, hauling coal trains to Ukraine and returning with empty wagons. He stayed at work until December that year.

One day, after returning home, his neighbours told him that 'visitors' from the new administration had been looking for him. It was likely that someone had reported him—because he had spoken openly to neighbours and others in the street, saying that what was happening was wrong, that it was illegal, and that the Russians were occupiers.

When the occupation began, society in Luhansk was sharply divided. Those who supported Ukraine called Russia what it was—an aggressor—and tried to explain to those welcoming the invasion that no pretext justified crossing a border and seizing another country's land. But others, including people Kostyantyn had once trusted—such as his children's godparents—dismissed it, saying it did not matter who ruled, who their neighbours were, or whether they were paid in roubles or hryvnias.

As a result, Kostyantyn and his family cut ties with many people they had once been close to. It was painful and disheartening. Ukraine had given those people everything, yet they betrayed their own country. Even now, he says, it still hurts to think about it—and to realise that people he knew could do such things.

* * *

Kostyantyn knew what it meant to be sought out by the Russian administration, so he hired a car and travelled to Mariupol to join his family. Once there, he went straight to the recruitment office to enlist, but was told that, as a freight train driver, he should continue working according to his profession—Ukraine needed workers.

Life in Mariupol suited the family. Kostyantyn recalled that the city was 'blooming like a flower'. When they had lived in Luhansk and visited Mariupol for holidays, it had seemed to them a rather grey, workmanlike place. But after the occupation of Luhansk in 2014, Mariupol grew into a city of regional importance, with significant investment. It became a vibrant, well-kept place with many new residential areas. No longer grey, it had turned into a multi-coloured city—and the majority of its people supported Ukraine.

Kostyantyn retired in 2017. He had told his wife that, because he had not joined the army in 2014, he would do so if Russia launched a real war, regardless of his age. When the full-scale invasion began on 22 February 2022, he was sixty years old. On 24 February, he went to the recruitment office.

* * *

On 24 February, Kostyantyn was at home when his wife rang from work and asked if he had switched on the television. He replied that he did not need a TV to know what was happening—the sounds of shelling and bombardment were already clear. When he did turn it on, he saw confirmation: a full-scale war against Ukraine had begun.

His wife told him she was coming home, as staff had been released from work. Kostyantyn answered that he was packing his duffel bag to head to the recruitment office. Before leaving, he embraced her. She said with a half-smile: 'Don't even think of not coming home! Just you try!' They laughed together, and then she added more softly: 'I will be waiting for you in Mariupol. But if we somehow lose each other, we'll meet in the fine city of Ivano-Frankivsk.'

There were many people in Mariupol who wanted to go to the front so there were long queues at the recruitment office. When Kostyantyn came there they told him that they couldn't recruit him as he was sixty and a half. 'What do you mean you can't recruit me?' Kostyantyn retorted. 'My two sons are fighting and I want to fight too.' So at the beginning they sent him to a detachment of border guards but the border guards said to him, 'Father, go home. We will manage.' Then Kostyantyn went back to the recruitment office and this time they decided to send him to a territorial defence detachment.

*   *   *

That was how Kostyantyn joined the 109th Brigade of Mariupol's territorial defence detachment, and from 25 February 2022 he was defending the city from the enemy. Russian air raids and explosions shook Mariupol, and his detachment moved to the Azovstal steel works. On 28 February they were sent to support the Azov Regiment.

Kostyantyn served as a sergeant and unit commander in the 109th Brigade. At that time, all senior commanders came from Azov, and those joining them were artillery. He began as an assistant grenadier, then became an assistant machine-gunner, and later a rifleman. Over the 86 days of Mariupol's defence, he mastered a range of military skills.

They were holding positions on the city's left bank. Commanders often told the men that reinforcements were on the way—and indeed, some help came, but it was limited. The Russians had concentrated enormous force on Mariupol, and from the second week the city was already under siege. The defenders soon understood that they could only rely on themselves. They would have to fight alone; no outside help could reach them.

Still, morale remained high. The fighters laughed, joked, and told stories. In the evenings they gathered to drink coffee together. Kostyantyn's heart ached at the sight of so many young men around him—most of them under thirty, some only 21 or 22. Many of them were killed. Yet no one cried, no one complained. They had been trained to fight.

Mariupol was ruined. The Russians burned the whole city. When they attacked Ukraine they had believed that they would be met with flowers. Perhaps they were told that people looked forward to their arrival because the people of Mariupol spoke Russian and watched Russian TV.

One day the reconnaissance soldiers came and said, 'We saw Russians taking toilet seats and carrying them away'. And they also heard Russians speaking over the radio saying: 'Why do they have such nice roads? We don't have such roads.' At the beginning the Russians used to shout: 'We don't fight with civilians. We are fighting with Azov.'

'Azov' was like a bone stuck in their throat. They wanted to destroy everything, to destroy the whole of Ukraine. The Russians saw that Ukrainians had a good life and were living in peace and comfort. They were jealous of that.

*   *   *

There were many children in Mariupol. When the defenders entered the basements of houses, they found them sheltering there in fear. Whenever the soldiers could, they gave the children a sweet or a piece of chocolate to cheer them. The children would hug and kiss their defenders, and draw pictures of doves and flags to give them as gifts.

These were patriotic drawings. Once a girl aged six or eight hugged Kostyantyn and said, 'Granddad, I am frightened.' She had a brother who was 14 years old. So Kostyantyn said to her, 'Look, your brother is so strong. Look, he is not crying. Take his hand and hold it tight. Don't lose each other. Stay together then you won't be frightened. Your brother will defend you.' The boy smiled at Kostyantyn and said: 'Yes, Granddad, I will defend her.'

*   *   *

There were lots of elderly people in the apartment houses. At the beginning when the defenders were cooking, they would bring potatoes and soup to the elderly. And the elderly too when they cooked something, they would bring their meals to the defenders: spring rolls, pancakes, patties. Practically every house in Mariupol was a fortress and that was why the Russians burned everything. The Russians would not look to see if there were any civilians in the house or not. The Russians would bombard the houses, boobytrap them, or destroy them with their tanks. And if the Russians knew that there were defenders in a house, they would burn it to cinders. When the situation became desperate, many civilians switched sides because they wanted to save their children.

From 28 February until 12 March, Kostyantyn fought on the front line under an Azov commander. At the end of March he was wounded for the first time, when a Russian sniper, aiming for his commander, missed and then turned his sights on him. The bullet struck Kostyantyn in the leg. Fortunately, the injury was not severe, and he was able to return to the front alongside his commander.

On 12 March the Ukrainian defenders were moving between positions. The morning began with shelling, followed by a Russian infantry assault, which the defenders managed to repel. After that, the Russians sent in a BTR armoured personnel carrier that set fire to the building. Kostyantyn only learned what had happened afterwards from his comrades, as he had no memory of it. When the Russian tank fired, he was buried under the ruins and remained unconscious for about six hours. His comrades dug him out after hearing his moans.

His injuries were grave: broken ribs, shrapnel in his arm and head, and damaged knees. A combat medic cleaned and dressed his wounds before transporting him to the hospital in Azovstal. Moving any wounded soldier to hospital was an enormous risk—the city was under constant bombardment, Mariupol lay in ruins, and everything was in full view of the enemy. Evacuations had to be carried out at night, as daytime brought the threat of snipers and missiles targeting any building in use. The men who carried out those evacuations were heroes, deserving the greatest respect and gratitude.

*   *   *

Kostyantyn received first aid at a hospital inside the Azovstal plant. By then, there was almost no food or medicine left. The Azovstal doctors seemed to have a gift from God Himself—they managed to save many wounded defenders without proper medication. Without them, countless lives would have been lost.

There were several hospitals within Azovstal, and Kostyantyn was taken to the central one. At that time it held around 350 severely wounded defenders, while those with lighter injuries remained on the front line to fight.

On 28 April came the heaviest shelling of all. The Russians destroyed the surgery, the canteen, and the main entrance of the central hospital. After that, the facility lay in ruins, with virtually no food or medicine. Not even painkillers. The surgeons were forced to operate without them.

Kostyantyn could no longer return to the front line, and he no longer had a weapon. The Azovstal plant was under siege, with defenders fighting on every approach. They formed a circle of defence, holding every side of the plant. It was relentless. Shelling rained down day and night. Aircraft attacked from above, and the Russians fired from their ships at sea. Yet the fighters held firm, declaring: 'I will not surrender. I will fight to the end!' Their spirit was unbroken, and everyone knew that those taking up combat positions would not allow the Russians to breach Azovstal.

There was no phone connection, no internet. The defenders had no way of knowing where their families were, or even if they were still alive. That uncertainty was the hardest burden to bear.

The wounded had only a radio, through which they learned that the whole world was speaking about Azovstal. Still, many believed they would die there, buried beneath its ruins. The bombardment was constant, with the Russians dropping ton after ton of bombs. The explosions shook everything. It was horrible.

Then the commander told the defenders that their commander in chief had ordered them to stop their resistance because the life of the soldiers was the most important thing. The defenders were told that they should come out. That was their destiny. They were told that they would be prisoners for three to four months only. On the 17th of May the list of the names of those who would have to leave with the first group was read out. Kostyantyn was in this group. They were led out. When the defenders approached the Russians, they were examined. The Russians took away the backpacks they liked, and then the Red Cross appeared—but no proper inspection was carried out. After that, the defenders were herded onto buses. Where were they being taken? Nobody knew. Captivity meant living in constant suspense. Once in the enemy's hands, you understood their cruelty.

This group of Mariupol defenders was taken to Olenivka.

It was horrific. Olenivka was Correctional Facility No. 120. Since 4 September 2014 it had been under the control of the unlawful, self-proclaimed Donetsk People's Republic, but the Russians later decided to use it to hold Ukrainian prisoners of war, turning it into a filtration camp.

When the defenders from Azovstal were brought there, they were subjected to thorough inspections. They were ordered to strip naked, every item was searched, and the Russians helped themselves to whatever they fancied. Kostyantyn had half a kilo of sugar—it was taken. If anyone protested, their belongings were simply cut to pieces.

The POWs were then crammed into a barrack built for 200 people, but packed with 525. There were no beds; prisoners had to sleep on the floor. A small, primitive stove stood in the corner, but there was no water supply. At first, water was brought in small 60–80 litre canisters; later the Russians installed 100-litre tanks. The water came from a lake, and the men had to drink it simply to avoid dying of thirst.

Food was almost non-existent. Just enough to keep them alive. If tea was given, it was no more than 100 grams, and without sugar. With no glucose, many fainted. A piece of bread weighing 100 grams had to last an entire day—sometimes even less. And it was never fresh, always stale. Meals consisted of prison soup: thin gruel with fish heads floating in it.

And over it all hung the constant threat of interrogation.

The interrogations followed a pattern. Typical questions were: 'Why did you join the army?' and 'Where did you serve?' The Russians were probing for weaknesses—trying to see who was strong and who might break, who might report on others and who would not.

Kostyantyn spent a month in Olenivka. Every day brought interrogations. Some prisoners were taken away, others left behind.

One day, the Russians read out a list of names and announced: 'Now you will go home.' What did that mean? Most men thought it was too good to be true, and assumed they were being moved elsewhere. They were right. Two hundred prisoners of war were transported instead to Luhansk Regional Prison.

When Kostyantyn joined the army, he had weighed 90–92 kilos. By the time he left Olenivka, he was down to just 55. Nearly half his body weight was gone.

In Luhansk Regional Prison, they were kept in a convict barrack, 200 men crammed together. When the Russians wanted to 'teach someone a lesson', they beat him mercilessly. Prisoners spoke of another punishment too: electric shocks. For this, men were ordered to put their hands behind their heads, bow low so they could not see their torturer, and stand with feet shoulder-width apart. Silence was enforced. If anyone raised his head, the guards struck it down.

The Russians needed no reason at all to beat a prisoner. Searches in the barracks were constant—everything would be turned upside down. Prisoners were forced to stand in the sun for hours and made to learn the Russian anthem, which was later tested. The guards looked at them with such hatred it seemed they were ready to tear them to pieces. That was how deeply they despised their captives.

Some prisoners testified that they were forced to give false evidence. The Russians repeated the same line again and again: 'Ukraine does not need you. Stay here in Russia. If you go back home, you will be put in camps and tortured for betraying Ukraine. You will be tried for treason.' An FSB officer interrogated Kostyantyn in exactly these terms. His reply was firm: 'I won't be arrested. I will be at home.'

During interrogations, the Russians also insisted that Ukraine was almost completely occupied. They told the prisoners that Lviv was already under Russian control. Later, they installed televisions and broadcast Russian news fronted by Olga Skabeyeva on a loop, 24 hours a day. What they failed to realise was that Ukrainians would not be deceived by propaganda. The prisoners sifted through the information, comparing it, drawing their own conclusions. They could work out what was true and what was false.

The Russians told them that Ukraine's allies had stopped supplying weapons. But the POWs knew the opposite was true. They did not believe that Kyiv or Lviv had been occupied—they understood that the Russians had not advanced beyond Donetsk. And when news came that Russia had 'tactically withdrawn' from Kherson, the prisoners knew what it meant: Kherson had been liberated. The joy was immense.

They could not cry out 'Hurrah!', but in low voices they sang the Ukrainian anthem. From their time in Olenivka, they knew exactly what punishment would follow if their torturers heard them sing in Ukrainian—especially the anthem.

On 6 March 2023 the prisoners of war were lined up and told: 'You have five minutes to get ready.' Most assumed they were being transferred to another prison—after all, exchanges from there were rare, and usually involved only one or two men at a time. But this time nearly 70 were assembled. When a Russian television journalist appeared and began asking questions about their life in Olenivka, the prisoners realised what it meant: they were going to be exchanged. It was almost impossible to describe what they felt. They wanted to believe the good news, yet hardly dared to.

On 7 March their hands were tied and they were blindfolded. The Russians took them to an airfield and flew them out. After landing, they were loaded onto buses, their hands untied and blindfolds removed, but they were ordered to keep their heads down and pull their caps over their eyes. Time dragged like an eternity. Finally, the bus stopped. The prisoners stayed motionless, waiting for orders. Then someone boarded and said: 'Guys, lift up your heads. You are home!'

Tears filled their eyes. Their souls were screaming. Kostyantyn pinched himself to check he was not dreaming. Volunteers rushed forward with Ukrainian flags, placing them in the hands of the Mariupol defenders. Everyone shouted: 'Glory to Ukraine!' Men embraced one another. For the first time, they knew with certainty that they had not been forgotten, that they had truly been freed from Russian captivity.

The feelings defied description. It was like being born again. And in that moment everyone understood: it had not been in vain. Not the fight, not the captivity, not the struggle to survive. None of it was for nothing.

Then the POWs were given mobile phones. That was their first conversation with their families since the 24th of February 2022. Kostyantyn's wife had found out for the first time that her husband was in Russian captivity in December 2022 when one of the other POWs was exchanged. Kostyantyn had given him his mobile number so he could phone Kostyantyn's wife and tell her that her husband was alive.

*   *   *

When Kostyantyn met his wife, she told him that she and kids had been under the Moskaly (Russian invaders) for a month and then they had walked on foot to Vuhledar, then reached Berdyansk by car. There the Russians had allowed a 'green corridor' and they went to Zaporizhzhia and from there volunteers helped them to travel to Ivano-Frankivsk.

*   *   *

Speaking later about his experiences, Kostyantyn admitted that returning to normal life after Russian captivity was extremely difficult. It felt as though he was home, yet he could not quite believe it. He did not want to talk to anyone—only to be left alone. After a year of war and imprisonment, the prisoners had become accustomed to that existence and almost fearful of freedom, which seemed so fragile.

Like all former POWs, Kostyantyn underwent treatment in hospital, supported by psychologists. He was treated in Lviv, where his wife came to visit him. Now aged 62, and left with wounds that prevent him from serving in the army, he has rejoined his family in Ivano-Frankivsk, where they have decided to settle.

In the city centre stands a Memory Alley dedicated to fallen heroes. For Kostyantyn, it is important to see how the residents honour their defenders—a constant reminder of the price Ukrainians pay for their right to be free. People here live their daily lives, but they also remember the sacrifices of servicemen. In Ivano-Frankivsk there are many soldiers, and locals show them respect: giving way to them in queues, or refusing payment for bus rides, even if they do not carry a 'Combat Veteran' certificate.

*   *   *

Ivano-Frankivsk is a quiet city, with friendly people. Kostyantyn's two elder sons are still serving in the army, fighting on the front line.

In the city, demonstrations are held in support of prisoners of war. These are not acts of resistance, but reminders—to show that the war continues, and that many defenders of Mariupol remain in captivity. Surviving in such inhuman conditions is extremely difficult, especially when the Red Cross seems absent and ineffective. This is an existential war, with brutal fighting. Some soldiers have been killed, others wounded, and many taken prisoner. Those held by Russia are tortured, beaten, starved, and left without medical care. The psychological strain is immense. They must be freed. They must be exchanged.

Everyone knows that the state is working on this. But prisoner exchanges are a two-way street, and the Russians use them in their own way. The Ukrainian government does great work on this front, and much of it has to be done in silence. That is why these demonstrations matter—they are reminders that our people are still in Russian captivity.

Kostyantyn himself was once a pro-Ukrainian, Russian-speaking man. Only now has he begun switching to Ukrainian. He has been learning for six months; though not yet fluent, he is determined to master it. His family has also changed to speaking Ukrainian. Their love for their country, he says, has grown a thousandfold.

*   *   *

As for the Russians, this nation doesn't exist for Kostyantyn any longer. And he wishes that the Russians would cease to exist for ever and ever. Kostyantyn would like to see huge walls built along the whole border of Ukraine and Russia, high walls so that Russians could not see or even hear Ukrainians. Let Russians stay in that enclosure and hang out with themselves. But unfortunately Russia doesn't want to leave Ukrainians alone.

They want to destroy us. No wonder that after razing Mariupol the Russians are now building new blocks of flats to sell to citizens of the Russian Federation—what hypocrisy. They claimed to be liberating Ukrainians, yet all they wanted was to colonise Ukraine. The same lies are told in Kharkiv, a largely Russophone city: missiles are aimed at civilians there under the pretext of 'liberating' Russians. The Russians kill children, the elderly, the disabled, and even pets with their missiles. They wipe out whole families. It does not matter to them that many of the victims speak Russian; their stated narrative of 'liberation' rings hollow. We know the truth, and we will not allow them to destroy Ukraine.

Young men of 19 or 20 still volunteer to fight for their country. Even after being captured and tortured, they tell us: 'We will come back and go to the front straight away. We will fight.' It is hard to put into words, but for Ukrainians the homeland—the land and the family—is sacred. We will overcome.

Source: Based on an interview by Suspilne News Ivano-Frankivsk 19 January 2024, filmed on Youtube https://www.youtube.com/watch?v=JbmkqBaf_Xs

Olexiy Anulya, the former Chernihiv kickboxing champion

This story shows what is really happening to Ukrainian prisoners of war in Russian captivity, and how completely the Russians ignore the Geneva Convention.

When the full-scale invasion began on 24 February 2022, Olexiy Anulya went straight to the recruitment office and volunteered to fight at the front. His father, a retired serviceman, also went there together with two of his former comrades—one a pilot, the other a submariner. Olexiy had urged his father to stay behind and help evacuate the family when the chance came, but his father insisted on fighting to defend his country.

Later, he was captured with another five or six wounded soldiers near a farm in the village of Lukashivka. Practically all the major Ukrainian formations were concentrated there—the 58th Brigade, the 16th Battalion, and the newly formed 21st Battalion. While tending to wounded Ukrainian soldiers, Olexiy's father was seized, and sadly tortured to death in a Russian chamber. His burnt body was found afterwards.

Olexiy himself, a machine gunner in the reconnaissance platoon of the 21st Rifle Battalion, fought his last battle before captivity in Lukashivka, Chernihiv region. There, his sworn brothers and fellow soldiers—Artem Sheremet, the second machine gunner in their unit, and Yuriy Vorona—were killed. It was also there that Olexiy hid his machine gun and the chevron of his fallen comrade Artem.

Olexiy Anulya took part in the battles for Lukashivka at the end of February and at the beginning of March 2022. The Russians managed to enter the village where

Olexiy and his nine comrades-in-arms were fighting and only Olexiy survived, though he was wounded.

Olexiy's unit had a different location from the other Ukrainian forces as they were in reconnaissance. The soldiers from the unit were exhausted as they had not slept for a long time. They desperately needed some rest. They found a forsaken house and decided to use it. Two women who were not from that village came to the house and asked if they needed anything. They also brought some borsch with them. But the soldiers did not have the chance to taste it for as soon as the women left the Russians started shelling their location mercilessly. It was obvious the Russians were targeting their position. Some civilians would give away the Ukrainian soldiers but others would hide them, give them food and shovels to dig trenches.

Olexiy and his friend Yuriy were still half-asleep when he suddenly saw a long white shell streak through the window. Both men leapt from their sleeping bags. Olexiy managed to throw himself out of a window, hitting the ground hard, and began crawling towards Artem Sheremet. Artem had already been fatally wounded in the neck.

Olexiy pressed his hands against the wound, trying desperately to stop the bleeding. Then another shell landed. The blast threw him into the ground. He was wounded and concussed. A bone was protruding from his right cheek, and part of a tooth was missing. His helmet had been torn in two.

Forty-nine fragments from the shell were embedded in the right side of his head, eight in his jaw, and four in his arm. His left ear rang with tinnitus while blood poured from the right.

When Olexiy turned back to Artem, his comrade's head was gone—only his body remained. Still, Olexiy felt for a pulse, clinging to hope. There was none.

Then Olexiy saw his friend Yuriy. He was sitting motionless on the steps of the house where they had been sleeping, his head bent forward. Olexiy crawled towards him, calling his name. There was no blood. He could not understand how Yuriy had died. His eyes were glassy. Olexiy reported to his commander that Yuriy had been killed, but to this day he still clings to a sliver of hope—that perhaps it had not been Yuriy at all, but someone else with those lifeless eyes.

Olexiy was the only survivor from his ten-man unit. Determined to fight on, he turned to the eight boxes of machine-gun ammunition still left. When he spotted the first MT-LB armoured vehicle about 400 metres away, he opened fire. Shock must have numbed him, and he fought with a 'come what may' resolve. The first MT-LB passed by, but he managed to destroy the second, emptying an entire clip from his Mossberg rifle. Seven boxes of ammunition still remained, but he no longer had the strength or the time to reload.

By then the Russian tanks were drawing closer. His first thought was: *What can I do next?*

There was no point in waiting for them. Olexiy ran, leapt the fence and hid in the high grass. From his concealment on the village outskirts he watched Russian tanks roll in, firing at houses, while infantry swept through, shooting the wounded. It became clear this was a clean-up operation: they took no prisoners—they killed everyone and finished off those who lay injured. Machine-gun bursts cracked around him as the soldiers searched for Ukrainian servicemen.

One tank drove straight towards his hiding place, its barrel trained on him. In that moment Olexiy thought it was the end. He slid his machine gun beneath his body, the barrel under his chin, and resolved he would pull the trigger if the Russians came close enough or stepped on him. He prepared himself to do it.

All he needed was to lie still in silence and gather his strength. He remained hidden for 12 hours, and by luck the enemy did not find him. At last he began to crawl from his hiding place, knowing that Russian checkpoints would already be scattered throughout the village.

He decided to conceal his documents, his machine gun, his chevron with the Ukrainian flag, and the ATO participant medal that had belonged to his fallen friend, Artem Sheremet. Then he knocked at the door of a house. For a long time there was no answer. He kept knocking. At last a woman opened, but she refused to let him in. There was a curfew in the village, and she did not recognise him. She had been helping Ukrainian soldiers during the fighting and could not believe he was still alive. Only after Olexiy gave her details that only she could know did she trust him.

It was a courageous act: in her home were her daughter with a baby, her son-in-law, and an elderly man. The family fed Olexiy and gave him mittens before he left again at night, crawling to a hamlet where his godfather lived. He reached it and hid in a tip near the cemetery, covering himself with paint tins and mineral wool. He slept for forty minutes.

When he woke it was eight in the morning. He set off running out of the village and passed the wrecks of tanks and armoured vehicles. But as soon as he left his hiding place, the Russians spotted him. He ran in the opposite direction, only to find more soldiers there. They were encircling him. He raised his hands and walked towards them.

A short Buryat soldier stepped forward. The others, machine guns levelled, closed in around Olexiy.

How Olexiy was captured by the Russians

'Who are you?'

'I am a local citizen.'

'Are you crazy? Why are you wearing Ukrainian uniform?'

'Really? It doesn't look like a uniform at all. We always wear overalls like this in the village.'

'Are you an idiot?'

Then they took off his hood and saw the wound on the right side of his head. So they took one step back and the Buryat aimed his machine gun at Olexiy.

'You are a Ukrop [*derogatory Russian slang term to refer to Ukrainian soldiers*]. We were fighting you all night. Where have you crawled out from?'

The soldier standing behind Olexiy struck him on the head with the butt of his rifle. He dropped to his knees as they began beating him with their guns and kicking him. Their aim was robbery, not capture. They took his knife, his mobile phone and his multitool. When they came to his tactical belt, which had 'Pentagon' written on it, they sneered: 'You're an American mercenary. Where did you learn to speak Russian without an accent?'

They looped the belt around him and dragged him across the road to a house Olexiy recognised instantly—it was his godfather's, where he had hoped to hide. Now the yard was filled with Russian military equipment. He was certain they were going to execute him.

For the first time in his life, Olexiy—who had never believed in God—began to pray, begging for salvation. His body was weak, his wounds aching, pain consuming him. He felt he had no strength left. Resigned to death, he asked his attackers to let him call his wife to say goodbye.

Just then the Russian commander of the unit appeared and asked, 'Who do we have here?' The soldiers answered: 'Comrade commander. Honestly, we were finishing off Ukrops all night and thought we'd got them all, but we don't know where this one has crawled from.'

At that moment Olexiy stood blindfolded, his hands tied behind his back, certain he was about to be executed. The commander, however, said: 'Hold on for a minute. I will call the general and ask what to do with this one.' The soldiers bundled him into an MT-LB, and Olexiy thought: this is only the beginning.

That was how he became a prisoner of war. Olexiy was held in Russian captivity from 10 March until 31 December 2022—roughly ten months. He spent the first six days in the Chernihiv region, then was taken into Russia. Two other POWs were with him: an officer and a warrant officer serving on contract. Within half an hour the Russians shot the Ukrainian officer; the warrant officer, aged around forty-five to fifty, was shot as well.

The captors found Olexiy's ATO medal. They pressed it to his forehead and began to kick him. Then they ripped off his chevron and jeered, 'You love Ukraine, don't you? Then eat this chevron.' Olexiy tried to obey; his torturers watched him closely. With his hands bound behind him, he could not hide the chevron, and his mouth was dry and bleeding. No matter how hard he tried, he could not chew the metal. Periodically they forced his mouth open to check. He could not speak, could not swallow—and worse torments lay ahead.

Attempt to rape Olexiy

'Now you will be punished for bombing Donbas,' they told him.

They forced Olexiy to the floor, face down. One Russian held him by the head to stop him moving, blood still seeping from his wound. They pulled down his trousers and tried to rape him.

'Did you wash your ass?' one asked.

Olexiy tried to reason with them, grasping at anything that might put them off.

'No. How could I? I was in the field. I went to the toilet there and wiped myself with a leaf.' He piled on the details, hoping to sicken them.

But when the Russian stripped him completely and straddled his calves, gripping his buttocks with his knees, Olexiy realised this was no game. He struggled to break free, but the man holding his head forced him still. Olexiy tried once more:

'You're against gay parades in Russia. You're against Europe.'

The reply was blunt: 'I don't care about that. I don't care about Putin. All I want is sex.'

At that moment gunfire erupted, shells landing close to the torture site. The Russians pulled him away, deciding to look for another victim. The next day Olexiy heard through the wall that they had raped someone else.

In the morning, he shouted that he needed to urinate. 'Everything is burning inside me,' he begged. The guard walked around, kicking him, and then sneered: 'Do your business where you are.' But Olexiy could not. His mind simply would not let his body go. Only later, perhaps by afternoon, he must have urinated, as he realised he had wet himself when he felt the warmth spread beneath him.

The torturers mocked him: 'Did you wet your pants?' As punishment they tied his hands behind his back with an extension cord fitted with an orange triple plug, and hooked it to the wall, and left him hanging there. He remained suspended like that for 24 hours, and then for another half day until evening. His hands swelled like boxing gloves. In agony, he screamed again that he needed to pee.

Finally a Russian soldier came and cut him down. Even he seemed shocked. 'Someone really thought this up?' he muttered, surprised at the cruelty of the method.

'Who did this to you?'

'I don't know. Perhaps it was you. I had my eyes covered.'

'Oh, no. It wasn't me. Perhaps those scumbags from Omsk.'

Then Olexiy understood that the soldiers in striped vests were paratroopers from Omsk.

Move to Kursk camp then Bryansk tent camp

After that Olexiy was brought to the Kursk camp, a disciplinary battalion in the Kursk region. He spent 12 days there. There were six Ukrainian soldiers transported with Olexiy.

Then they were moved to Bryansk. Luckily for Olexiy there was a Russian man called Sergei there who recognized Olexiy for his sports success. When Sergei was taking Olexiy to the toilet he said: 'I care about your life.'

And it was Sergei who helped and supported Olexiy in captivity. Actually Sergei made arrangements for Olexiy to be taken to the tents. He said: 'It will be difficult but you will survive.' It was also Sergei who gave Olexiy his checkered underpants. Then the head of the guard, nicknamed Ratnik, who was extremely cruel and a racist, said: 'Look at this one. He is very dangerous. He took these underpants from a Russian soldier. He will be under my personal control.' It was that Ratnik who made Olexiy kneel outside the tent in the snow and he who ordered two of Olexiy's teeth be pulled out. This was because Olexiy had killed Russian soldiers.

The prisoners were given just one minute to eat. Olexiy, with his injured jaw, could not chew quickly enough. He hid a piece of bread for himself and for a helicopter pilot with a broken spine, who could not walk outside the tent to collect his own meals. As they left the canteen, Olexiy was still chewing. A guard noticed, grabbed him by the collar, and dragged him to their checkpoint.

Olexiy knew that if they discovered the hidden bread it would mean severe punishment for the entire tent—the Russians would beat them all to death. So he stuffed the bread into his mouth and chewed as fast as he could.

He was taken to another tent in a field and ordered to kneel. Two guards sat nearby eating sunflower seeds and began spitting the husks onto him. Olexiy was unshaven, with a thick beard, when suddenly a dentist emerged from the tent and barked: 'Where have you been? I've been waiting for you for an hour and a half.'

The Russians dragged him inside and ordered him to strip. Naked, he was led into the medical room. The dentist asked, 'What do you need treated?'

'Nothing, he doesn't need treatment,' one of the guards replied. 'Just pull out two molars.'

The dentist hesitated. 'I can't do that. I swore the Hippocratic Oath.'

From the corner of his eye, Olexiy saw the nurse trembling. Perhaps, he thought, there was still something human left in them. 'Do you feel sorry for him?' one of the guards asked.

The dentist replied, 'Shall I inject lidocaine?'

'What for?' the guard snapped. 'He'll be shaking all over afterwards.'

That was the end of it.

The dentist switched on his headlamp and directed the light at Olexiy, who lay trembling from the cold and from dread of what was to come. He was ordered to close his eyes. The dentist pulled out one tooth next to the canine and then the wisdom tooth—breaking off part of the jawbone in the process. As he worked, he muttered, 'Why don't you brush your teeth? You're wounded, you need to keep up your hygiene.'

Then he switched off the headlamp and asked quietly, 'Do you understand where you are?'

'I am in captivity,' Olexiy answered.

'Forgive me,' the dentist said.

Olexiy bore him no grudge. He understood that the man had tried, in his own way, to lessen the suffering—even though the experience had been hellish. His mouth filled with blood.

The dentist held up the teeth for the guards to see. 'Is that enough?' he asked.…

One of them, still smoking, shrugged. 'OK, that will do.'

Kursk SIZO (pre-trial detention centre)

Later, Olexiy was transported to Kursk—to SIZO No. 1. He remained there for forty days.

The *priyomka*—the routine of inspection and admittance—lasted seven hours. The SIZO itself was a living hell. Olexiy was beaten so savagely that his entire body turned blue and purple. His nose was broken, his right eye badly damaged. The haematomas were so severe he could not even go to the toilet. In the bathhouse, where the beatings continued, one of his vertebrae was broken; later, another was fractured too.

He was then placed in a cell meant for four prisoners but crammed with twelve. Extra bunks had been welded above the first row to form a second tier. Even so, there was not enough space for everyone to stand at once.

Interrogations by counterintelligence and the FSB followed a set pattern. The POWs were first dragged into the corridor, where the beatings began. Blows rained down indiscriminately. The Russians did not care what they broke—kneecaps, spines, ribs, ligaments. It made no difference to them whether the prisoner was a civilian, a woman, a soldier, someone elderly or mentally ill.

Meals were meagre. In the mornings the prisoners were given a thin porridge made with water, or overcooked pasta, or broken rice. This was considered a 'hearty' meal. It came with half a small glass of water and a piece of bread—thick but porous, with almost no calories.

Lunch was even worse: a watery prison soup, little more than boiled water with a single cabbage leaf floating in it. There was never any meat or potatoes. The 'main course' was chopped rice or buckwheat chaff—not real grain, just husks. Lunch was served at four o'clock in the afternoon, which meant enduring hunger from six in the morning when breakfast was given.

Dinner brought sprouting potatoes, and fish waste: boiled intestines, tails and bones ground into a paste. The guards liked to sneer: 'Our dogs wouldn't eat this. We give them meat. Do you want some meat from our dog's bowl?'

Easter beatings

When Easter came, one guard asked if the prisoners would like an egg. They replied that they would be very grateful—they were all Orthodox Christians. 'You'll get it in the evening,' the guard said.

At Easter lunch they received nothing more than a cabbage leaf with boiling water poured over it. There was no main course—it was worse than usual. Olexiy ate the leaf and felt a surge of energy. Imagine how weak a person must be to feel revived by a single boiled cabbage leaf. In that moment, Olexiy believed a cabbage leaf could decide his life. Just a leaf.

In the evening, they were given another cabbage leaf for dinner. Olexiy dared to ask the guard on duty: 'And what about the Easter egg you promised us?'

'All in good time. Don't worry, you'll get it. Everything comes to those who wait,' the guard replied.

At eight o'clock that evening, during the routine 'evening examination,' the POWs were led from their cells into the corridor. Russian Special Forces, including Buryats as well as local units, were waiting. They greeted one another as the prisoners' unease grew. Something was about to happen.

Then the beatings began. The guards struck the POWs in the groin, jeering: 'Well, here's what you wanted, isn't it? You wanted eggs.' After that attack, Olexiy felt certain he would not survive much longer.

Strict Regime Camp, Tula Region

From Kursk pre-trial detention centre, Olexiy was transported on 5 May 2022 to the village of Donskoye in Tula region. It was a strict regime camp. From 5 May until 20 August, he was held in cell number 20. Then, from 20 August until 31 December, he was transferred to punishment cell number one. He spent 108 days there.

When new prisoners arrived, the Russians ordered them out three at a time. The men were forced to run into the camp yard, where guards stood lined up on both sides, forming a 'live corridor.' The POWs had to jump and stumble their way across before reaching a building where the *priyomka* began once again. Another *priyomka*. Always another. They were beaten, stripped to ensure they carried nothing, registered by name, and then assigned to cells.

Olexiy's wounds had not even begun to heal from the earlier beatings, yet here the process was repeated.

In the cells, the men were given one jerrycan for urine between them all. If one man relieved himself fully, the others would have nowhere to go. The can filled quickly. To avoid anyone being forced to drink urine to make space, each man tried to urinate only a little, so that all would have their turn.

Olexiy remembers his cellmates' faces: the border guard from Chernihiv region he had befriended in Kursk; Oleksandr Antonenko from Kotsyubynske; an old man; and two other men transferred from Kursk. Their faces were pale, grey—like corpses. Every prisoner lived with the same feeling: the expectation that something bad was about to happen.

The POWs were sorted according to their medical conditions—for example, those with leg wounds, holes torn through their limbs. In Olexiy's cell there were three others. One was a marine from Mariupol, who had lost his son at the Illich Steel Plant, part of Azovstal, before being taken prisoner himself. Another was from Volnovakha, a civilian who had once supported Russia. For him it was especially bitter: he had loved Russia, yet here he was, beaten daily like everyone else.

Beatings came every day, sometimes several times a day. When Olexiy, because of his leg injuries, sat down on his bed, a camera flash went off instantly and a voice shouted: 'Why did you sit down? Did you hear the order? Stand up, you son of a bitch! Hands up! To the bars, head down!'

He had to remain like that until evening. No further order came. At last he said, 'I have an injured leg. Can I sit down?'

The reply was immediate: 'I don't care. That's your problem.'

Later, a hatch opened in the wall and a young Special Forces soldier stepped inside. 'You, the young one—come here. Are you a kickboxer? Who do you know in kickboxing?'

Olexiy gave him some names from Orel, and the Russian seemed satisfied— perhaps he recognised them. Olexiy allowed himself a flicker of hope: maybe this man might help him, might somehow contact his family and let them know he was alive.

In the end it was Sergei from Bryansk who managed to reach out. He called his wife, who then created a special account so she could pass news to Olexiy's wife. By then, though Olexiy did not know it, his wife was already aware that he was a prisoner of war.

The following day, the same Special Forces soldier took several POWs for a walk in the yard. At first everything seemed calm. As they walked, however, they could hear the screams of other prisoners being beaten inside the building. Still, those in the yard were left untouched, even permitted to do some light exercises—though they were forbidden to lift their heads.

Olexiy noticed the Special Forces patch on the Russian's cap: 'BARS.' He also spotted an officer from the military commissariat, held in cell number 16. His name was Borysenko, from Izyum. Among them too was a man from Kharkiv, from the 92nd Brigade—Olexiy's friend, a truly decent person. But Borysenko betrayed him.

His friend had been planning an escape, but Borysenko gave him away. He was thrown into a punishment cell. Nobody would ever want to see Borysenko return to Ukraine. He handed over everything he knew to the Russians: the locations of recruitment offices in Kharkiv, the metro stations, and more.

For two days after *priyomka* the POWs were given nothing to eat. Then came cabbage—so overcooked and oversalted that Olexiy, despite his hunger, could not force it down. His stomach burned. The following day brought porridge cooked in water, not milk, with a piece of white bread. Lunch was half a plate of thin soup, a small main course, and even a few pieces of fried lard with bread. Supper was cabbage, bread, and a piece of herring. Everyone was astonished. Olexiy thought to himself: *Not bad. You could survive on this.*

But it lasted only four days. After that, rations were drastically reduced, often little more than water.

On 9 May the prisoners were taken outside for a walk. It was snowing heavily, and they were soon drenched and shivering. They had only slippers on their feet, and their prison uniforms were thin and flimsy. In the cells, the cold was constant. Their hands turned blue with freezing, and in the mornings, when ordered to wash, they could not even manage it—their hands were too numb. Draughts cut through the cells, and when prisoners were made to stand, they were forbidden to move.

When Olexiy returned from the walk, the cell door opened. 'Anulya, leave the cell,' came the order. He was taken to a room, bent over, and beaten. Seven Special Forces soldiers struck him, with two more standing behind. As they hit him, they fired questions: 'Where was Krasnoyartsev? Who shot him down? Where was he hiding?'[1]

Olexiy told them he was just a driver, that he could not possibly have shot the pilot down. But his torturers would not believe him. They seemed to think Ukraine was just one big village where everyone knew everyone else. For Olexiy it was hard to fathom such ignorance in the 21st century.

In fact, the interrogations were almost always the same, wherever he was held. Questions about his attitude to the war. About Crimea. About the so-called People's Republics of Donetsk and Luhansk. About whether he had taken part in the Maidan Revolution. About whether he knew anyone from Azov, the Right Sector party or the Aidar Battalion, and what he thought of them. They even wanted to know his views on the church split between the Ukrainian and Russian Orthodox, and which church he attended. One FSB officer even phoned Chernihiv Trinity Church to check whether Olexiy was a parishioner. Questions about the church came up at practically every interrogation.

They also obsessed over how Olexiy spelt his name—with an 'O' rather than the Russian 'A.' They could not grasp that Ukrainian was a different language. When Olexiy wrote down dictated texts and inserted commas, they were astonished. 'How do you know where to put commas?' they asked. Olexiy explained simple grammar rules, like placing a comma before 'but.' The Russians pressed him: 'Where did you get your education?'…

---

1   Krasnoyartsev was a Russian pilot shot down over Chernihiv in March 2022, later returned to Russia in a prisoner exchange, and sentenced in absentia by a Ukrainian court for murdering a civilian in Chernihiv.

'At school,' he replied.

The idea of a university education seemed extraordinary to them. Even some of the Russian officers had never been to university. By contrast, practically all the Ukrainians in captivity were educated men. All had finished school, and many had degrees.

They beat Olexiy with clubs like those used by Berkut and OMON. The rubber ones left swelling and bruises, but the plastic sticks were worse: they split the skin, cut deep into muscle, and left wounds that festered. On top of that came stun guns and gas canisters. Guards sprayed gas directly into prisoners' faces or sometimes filled entire cells with it.

Each shift seemed to invent its own tortures, but one in particular stood out as especially sadistic. They forced prisoners to squat constantly, even inside their cells, then made them shuffle squatting from the first floor to the second and back again—300, sometimes 500 squats at a time. No sooner had one order been carried out than another began.

The guards monitored everything on CCTV. God forbid a prisoner's squats were too shallow, or a group fell out of sync while squatting in formation with arms on each other's shoulders. One mistake, one 'wave' in the movement, and punishment followed immediately. 'Didn't you hear the order? Think you're cleverer than the rest?' they shouted—before laying into them again.

The aim was to break someone—to find the weakest link. Every time a prisoner left his cell, he knew exactly what awaited him: more beatings, more humiliation. Hearts raced with dread, but the one thing you could not allow was for the guards to see your fear. They thrived on it. A scream or a terrified look sent them into fits of laughter. 'We are the best. We are the Marine Corps, the elite,' they boasted.

One guard in particular, known as Vados, was their ringleader. Tall, muscular, built like a bull, he barked commands as if training dogs. He devised a system of knocks on the cell doors. One knock—the prisoners had to shout, 'Good day, Boss!' Two knocks—a formal report: 'Boss, cell number twenty. Number of detainees: ... Report given by cell duty prisoner Anulya Olexiy Yevhenovich.' Three knocks meant squats.

Four knocks meant shouting 'Pika-pika-choo!' in a childish singsong, drawing out the final 'chooo' as though they were nursery kids. Five knocks required chanting insults about Ukraine's president and America's president: 'Zelensky is a faggot. Biden is a faggot.' Six knocks meant chanting: 'Whoever is not jumping is a Russian, whoever is jumping is a faggot!'—all while they were forced to jump, watched hawk-like and berated for not jumping high or hard enough.

Seven knocks meant shouting: 'Russia is a generous soul.' The guards played this knocking game constantly, especially with newcomers. They would rap on different doors at different times—one knock on Olexiy's cell, two on the next—making it almost impossible to tell which command applied to which cell.

The key was instant response. Everyone in the cell had to shout the prescribed words in perfect chorus. If one or two voices came in too early or too late, it was enough to trigger punishment. To Olexiy, it felt like conditioning, like being trained as Pavlov's dogs.

Even something as ordinary as a haircut became another form of torture. While one prisoner was having his hair cut, another would be beaten—and then they would switch places. The barber's hands shook so badly under the pressure that he often nicked the scalps of those in his chair. Everyone understood the grim calculation: the longer the barber worked, the longer another prisoner endured his beating.

The barber was an elderly man. That day, Olexiy was first. Ordered to remove his shirt, the guards noticed the trace of muscle on his thin frame. 'Do you work out?' they demanded. In truth, Olexiy did try to exercise secretly in his cell, though it was forbidden.

At the same time, another prisoner—a professional basketball coach—was stripped and savagely beaten. Olexiy could hardly bear it, knowing that every moment his hair was being trimmed meant more blows for his comrade. And he also knew he would be next.

When the cut was finished, Olexiy was forced to thank the barber with the words: 'Thank you, Nikolaevich, the best barber ever.' Then the guards turned on him. They beat him so brutally that he had to crawl nearly ten metres down the corridor back to his cell. Soon after, he was dragged again—this time to the punishment block, Cell Number One.

Olexiy had kept his previous cell so clean that the Russians mockingly called it 'the Euro suite.' Later they told him that because he had lived in a 'suite cell,' he now had to 'pay' for it. His punishment was to be moved into a cell that was little more than a cesspit.

The floor was covered with a thick layer of faeces. Almost every inch of the walls was black with mould. The stench was unbearable. Behind the cell lay a cesspool into which the excrement from twenty other cells drained. It leaked through, leaving a foul black sediment on the floor. Olexiy knew it was only a matter of time before he contracted tuberculosis.

And then there was the dripping. From the moment he entered, water dripped constantly, endlessly, an assault on his mind as much as his body. It gnawed at him until it felt as though his brain might split apart.

The cell itself was tiny—just enough space for a bed, a nailed-down table, a chair, a washstand, and a hole in the floor that served as a toilet. The only free space was a small square where you might put a chair.

Two men from the Russian penitentiary service had moved Olexiy there after finding a small piece of soap hidden in his belongings. That scrap of soap, given to him months earlier, was his treasure—he used it to brush his teeth. For this, he was beaten savagely and thrown into the punishment cell.

From then on, each day followed the same pattern: dragged from the cell, beaten without mercy, then dumped back into the stinking hole. Once, they even 'set a record,' as they called it, thrashing him for two and a half hours. A few Special Forces men tried to intervene, but it made no difference. The beatings continued.

Lying there half-conscious, Olexiy heard one of his torturers mutter, 'I'm tired of beating him—my arm's sore.' Another answered, 'Let me do it.' When they finally threw him back into the punishment cell they sneered: 'Why does it stink all the time? Don't you flush the toilet? You've got two minutes to make the cell smell of lilies of the valley—and get rid of that bit of soap.' So Olexiy was forced to try to scrub the floor with that tiny scrap of soap, though it was useless against the thick layer of faeces.

After his move to the punishment cell his rations were cut dramatically and he was almost constantly starving. He begged for food but was given only two spoons of prison soup and a piece of bread. He and the man in the next punishment cell were wasting away. Once, after forcing down those two spoonfuls and the bread, he began to shake uncontrollably: an icy cold spread over his face and the back of his head, his eyes rolled, and a terrible thought crossed his mind—'Mother... I don't think I'll get through this. I won't survive.' He collapsed; his nose ran so heavily, and he thought that his body did not have the strength to digest the bread.

The prisoners were taken out to the yard for a walk. The ground was paved with uneven concrete slabs, tilted at odd angles, with tufts of grass growing between them. It was there, in the grass, that Olexiy spotted a large worm.

Bruised, shaking, his clothes streaked with whitewash, he bent down, picked it up and slipped it into his mouth. Just then a guard came near to march him back to the punishment cell. Again came the same order: clean the cell, make it smell of lilies of the valley—they would be back to check.

Olexiy did not swallow the worm straight away. He wanted to save it. He wrapped it in a floorcloth and left it by the toilet tank, where water dripped constantly. Soon after, he was taken out for another beating. By the time he returned, he had forgotten about it.

A week later, while wringing out the floorcloth to stop water from spreading across the cell, he found it: the big worm had produced a brood. Tiny worms, just two centimetres long, wriggled inside the damp cloth. There were plenty of them. The large worm itself was shrivelled and near dead, but Olexiy ate the young ones— and kept the big worm aside, hoping it would breed again and provide another meagre meal.

That same evening the pangs of hunger became unbearable and Olexiy could not resist—he ate the large worm too. It did not satisfy him, but somehow it felt like meat; he told himself he had taken a few extra calories and, if he had survived yesterday, he could survive tomorrow. He convinced himself he would have enough energy to last another half-day after that.

Starvation drove him to try anything. He nibbled at a sliver of laundry soap, only to be seized by terrible stomach pains and a burning sensation inside; foam came from his mouth. He chewed on the little remaining toilet paper—there was hardly any— and even tore open a 30-gram tube of toothpaste, long past its use-by date, and ate the sugary paste with his finger. It was a type of carbohydrate; he hoped it would keep him going until morning.

Then he planned his next move. Rather than trying to fill his stomach with water, as people usually do, he decided he needed to slow his digestion—to do the opposite—so that the little he had eaten might last longer.

Back in Cell Number 20, just above the punishment block, Olexiy had once tried to hunt a rat. He saw it darting along the corridor but it never ventured down to his cell. He tried every trick he could think of to lure it in, but he could not bring himself to part with even a crumb of his bread. That daily piece was life itself. He ate it slowly, crumb by crumb, savouring each morsel. He needed every fragment for his own survival.

He doubted he would ever have the strength to strangle the rat anyway; his fingers cramped constantly. Still, he had noticed a nail protruding near the toilet hole, sticking up out of the faeces, and thought perhaps it might serve as a weapon if the chance ever came.

By December, men from the FSB came to see him. It was bitterly cold. To keep warm in his cell, Olexiy would wrap himself in his bed sheet, tying it in a knot around his stomach. He pulled it tight across his chest, crossed it behind his back, sucked in his stomach—though at 62 kilos there was little left to suck in—and tied it fast. Over this he wore his underwear, then the thin prison uniform, before forcing himself to do squats to warm his body.

That day, one of the guards, a torturer named Ischenko, appeared on shift. 'So, finally, we've got this man in Punishment Cell Number One,' he sneered. Olexiy gave the required report, was hauled out, and searched. They found nothing. Then they noticed the knot in his sheet

'What's that?'

'My kidneys are sick in the draught...'

'Oh, I see.'

Olexiy found the reaction strange. Suddenly the Russians seized him by the neck, marched him down to the first floor and into the interrogation room opposite Cell 20. He saw six pairs of feet and knew beatings were coming. They forced him to sit and to lift his head. Then Ischenko and his men left the room.

When he looked up, an FSB officer was there. 'What can I say to you?' the man began. 'I see you like to break the rules.' He went on to tell Olexiy that his being in a punishment cell was not accidental: his wife had learned he was a prisoner because someone in Russia had managed to contact her. They had discovered who had passed the information on. The FSB warned them not to interfere—or they would 'lose everything.' According to the officer, there was a list of Ukrainian POWs drawn up in Moscow, and Olexiy's name was the only one Moscow forbade them to exchange.

The officer produced four and a half sheets of paper listing prisoners' names. Some were highlighted in yellow, some in orange—and on the second sheet Olexiy's name alone was highlighted in grey.

They led him back to the punishment cell, beating him on the way, and flung him inside by his shirt. He was ordered to stand without moving. In that moment Olexiy thought it was the end. He decided he would hang himself. But before he tried, he wrote a poem for his mother—a last farewell. In it he used 'wine glasses' for the prison mugs and called the guards 'watchdogs.'

Farewell Poem to My Mother
There are walls, plank-beds, wooden floors and wine glasses
And I am standing there for seventeen hours and waiting for the watchdog's command
I wished so much for a different life,
A green meadow is growing around my dacha
And I am standing at the barbecue frying meat
My woman is next to me,
And children are running in the garden,
And we are all screaming with laughter,
The sun is shining, everything is as it should be,
And everything is fine with me.
The ways of God are mysterious
Wounds of your soul are not the wounds of your body,
And as we all know now, all actions have a price,
I am standing here behind the bars,
Yelling at the top of my voice in silence, but there is just no point in that.
My life has ended here,
Oh well, evil fate, you broke my life to pieces,
The sheet is tightening a noose around my neck like a snake
My heart is no longer beating in my chest.
My mother is not laughing anymore.
When will this war suck enough of young men's blood?

Olexiy was trying to hang himself.

Believing he had no choice, Olexiy had fashioned a noose from his bedsheet and prepared to hang himself. There was not enough height to drop, so he planned to fall on his knees; he slipped his head through the loop and, as he was about to tighten it, a vision came to him—his granny, his father's mother, the last relative to die before his father. She walked slowly round the washstand in the cell and seemed to say, 'Look at what he is about to do. It's too early—you haven't chosen New Year presents for your children yet.'

For a moment he could not tell whether he was hallucinating or awake. The guards did not notice anything on the surveillance cameras, so they peered through the hatch and saw a white sheet hanging. They rushed in, loosened the noose and hauled him out. They searched him again, then ordered him to lift his shirt and began to beat his right kidney. That side of his body was already mottled purple; the Russian struck it methodically, sneering, 'You can live on one kidney. You don't need two. You will live on pills for the rest of your life.'

Olexiy was furious with his grandmother's vision—she had denied him the chance to end it all. With no hope left, he began to pray....

'Dear God, if there is even one per cent chance of me getting out of here, give me a sign.'

At that very moment, he saw a rat.

He never knew how it managed to get into the cell, but it scurried in through a gap near a roof beam, searching for scraps. Starving and desperate, Olexiy lunged like an animal and caught it in his hands. It was only a young rat, smaller than he had hoped—hardly any meat. Still, he thought of splitting it open to eat from the inside, using the nail near the toilet hole.

He tore a piece of skin, but the rat writhed violently, fighting for its life. Then he heard the wardens approaching—perhaps he had disappeared from their camera view and they were coming to check. The door opened. Without hesitation, Olexiy shoved the rat into his mouth and bent down, trying to hide it.

He could not report his name as required; with the rat between his teeth, his tongue was bitten at the tip in two places and the roof of his mouth torn. He tried to speak, but it was impossible. The guards laughed. 'What's wrong? Forgotten your name?' They beat him on the knees and the back of the head as he shielded his eyes with his hands.

Then one noticed thick, dark blood dripping from his mouth onto the floor. 'Ah, that's better,' the guard said. 'Take him away.'

They dragged him back to the punishment cell and ordered him to stand at attention. He missed dinner that night, but he didn't care—he was chewing the rat. For him, it was meat.

Olexiy chewed the rat down to the bones. The fur clung between his teeth, the intestines stuck too, but he told himself the meat was full of calcium and protein. He gnawed even at the skin. It took a long time to break down, but when saliva gathered in his mouth he thought it better to keep chewing rather than swallow—it might trick his body into feeling full for longer.

In truth, he never felt full at all. Yet somewhere deep inside he believed he had eaten meat, that it balanced out the thin carbohydrates in the prison soup, and that it would give him the strength to last until morning.

Through it all, the tune of Jingle Bells circled endlessly in his mind—it had been playing there for two weeks. He no longer dreamed of escape; he knew it was impossible. Instead, his thoughts turned to home, to what presents he might give his wife and children for New Year, and to how he would spend those moments with them.

Exchange

On 28 or 29 December, the day began like any other. But that morning there was no walk in the yard. From 9 a.m. the Russians started calling prisoners out of their cells. The order 'Take your *skatka*'—a bedroll with a mattress and belongings rolled inside—meant a move to another cell. The order 'Leave your *skatka*' could mean transfer to another camp, or, with luck, an exchange.

That day they took Olexiy again. He was led to what they called the 'Tapik.' It was nothing more than an old wooden chair with a fitting above the head. The guards soaked his body with foam, clamped wires to his nipples and chest, and pulled a cap over his head.

There were two settings of current they used. The first was so strong it would knock Olexiy unconscious. He would see only a white corridor, then be revived with ammonia while his torturers went outside for a cigarette—not just for five minutes, but for half an hour, sometimes forty minutes—before returning to start again.

The second setting was weaker but continuous, a steady current that never let up. For Olexiy, this was worse: a relentless, searing pain, like an unending electric shock coursing through his body.

After the torture, the Russians dragged Olexiy out. His legs were giving way beneath him; he could barely walk. A young guard decided to climb onto his back, riding him like a horse. Each time Olexiy collapsed, he was forced to get up again, only for the guard to jump back on. In this way they drove him down the corridor, where at the far end Olexiy saw a group of Special Forces men waiting.

They ordered him to strip naked and then to dress again—not in his own clothes, but in another prisoner's soiled underwear, already stiff with dried faeces. Over it he was given a reeking blue shirt and a pair of thin synthetic trousers. Later, when he was transported in the prison van, he noticed two holes in the fabric, with a dried tendon stuck to them. The trousers were stained with vomit and blood, and stank. On top he had to wear a filthy civilian jacket.

Finally, they gave him shoes. By sheer luck, they were his own. Inside, still hidden, was the small voodoo doll he had made from threads, a figure he had named *Shredder*. He had made it to have someone to speak to, so as not to lose his mind, and had hidden it in his shoes knowing the guards would have destroyed it if they'd found it in his cell. Against all odds, he kept it—and brought *Shredder* home with him.

The Russians brought the prisoners into a room, where Olexiy recognised several men he had known from Kursk prison. They were told they were to be executed, shot on the spot. But the threat was a lie. The Russians never told the POWs that they were to be exchanged.

Instead, they were taken to the exchange point—an open field with no checkpoints. There, food was handed to them: apples, yoghurts, and children's drawings. Olexiy carried those drawings with him throughout his rehabilitation. The prisoners were afraid to eat, their stomachs too fragile to cope after months of starvation, yet the food was irresistible, almost unbearably delicious.

From there, they were driven to Sumy. It was night, and the city lay in darkness. The POWs were taken straight to hospital. When the surgeon saw Olexiy, he immediately ordered staff to put him in a wheelchair—his legs were grotesquely swollen, like those of an elephant, with open holes seeping pus. Olexiy protested that he could still walk, but the surgeon insisted.

An X-ray was taken. The results were stark: Olexiy's legs were literally peeling, the skin separating from the bone. He was emaciated, 38 kilograms lighter, skeletal in frame yet carrying legs ballooned with infection. The surgeon asked him:

'Do you know what is happening to you?'

'Probably a lack of vitamins,' Olexiy replied.

'No,' the surgeon said. 'You were kept in the cold. This is a method of torture. The Nazi fascists were the first to devise it. The cold makes the skin exfoliate—your legs become like a three-dimensional model.'

When Olexiy went to shower, the warm water caused his legs to swell even more. Afterwards, he tried to climb the stairs to his room, but just a metre from the door his legs gave way completely. He could not make it inside.

The next morning Olexiy's family came to see him. He saw his brother, his wife, and his closest friend. His little son did not recognise him. When Olexiy had gone to the front, the boy was just two years old; now he was five. His daughter did recognise him, but she was frightened by his appearance.

Before the war, Olexiy had stood 1.93 metres tall and weighed 100 kilograms. When he was released from Russian captivity, he was 1.86 metres tall and weighed just 62 kilograms. The doctors diagnosed concussion, damage to the sella turcica [a saddle-shaped depression in the skull housing the pituitary gland], and brain injuries, including a cerebral haematoma. Fortunately, he narrowly avoided trepanation (a medical procedure involving the drilling of a hole in the scull to relieve intercranial pressure).

His list of injuries was devastating: a broken nose, a shattered jaw, multiple broken fingers—some in two places—two broken collarbones, and a shoulder blade now jutting out. His spine bore three consolidated fractures, his tailbone had been broken a day before the exchange, and his ribs and rib cage were badly damaged. His organs carried the trauma of repeated beatings. He had suffered six untreated concussions.

Since his release, Olexiy has been treated in 16 hospitals, yet he has not fully recovered. He still requires another operation on his jaw to replace the teeth that were pulled out. Some injuries cannot be repaired: his right kidney, beaten beyond saving, is lost. He can no longer train at a high level, and doctors have advised that the bicycle and the swimming pool must be his lifelong companions.

Even so, Olexiy carries a powerful motivation: his children.

Olexiy was a multiple champion of Ukraine in kickboxing. He won both the Ukrainian Cup and the CIS Cup (Commonwealth of Independent States) and was crowned elite fighting champion of the CIS in 2013. He retired from professional sport at just 22, already married and with a daughter. Afterwards, he worked as a bodyguard abroad in Austria—a job that demanded not only peak physical fitness but also sharp intelligence.

Now, Olexiy is thinking about becoming a trainer. Almost all the men he once knew from the gym are serving in the Ukrainian armed forces, and he wants to be a role model not only for his own children but also for the boys in his neighbour-hood. It pained him when his wife took their son to the local gym and found no one there to train him—all the coaches had gone to the front. But before anything else, Olexiy knows he must recover from his own many injuries. He is also considering work on rehabilitation programmes for military personnel. His aim is to be useful, to find fulfilment in helping others. He has seen countless servicemen returning from the frontline who cannot bring themselves to trust doctors or therapists with no mili-tary background. Olexiy believes he can reach them, especially those who, like him, survived Russian captivity. He has already drawn up a list of men he thinks he can help.

So far, Olexiy has managed to assist ten prisoners in returning home, often working alongside their mothers. He informed the relevant institutions where these captives were being held and described the dire conditions they faced. At the same time, he is collaborating with international organisations to raise awareness. What troubles him deeply is that those most in need—the prisoners in the worst condition—are often not prioritised for exchange. This weighs heavily on him. Olexiy still struggles with sleep and is haunted by dreams of the men left behind. For him, it is impossible to live a normal life knowing that Ukrainian POWs are still dying in Russian prisons. At present, he is working to help twelve more captives. But in his heart, he is already plan-ning for many others who, he believes, must be freed from the Russian death camps.

Olexiy still thinks about the day he will return to Russia to face his torturers and look them in the eye. He despises them and wants them to pay for what they did—so that their descendants will be afraid to do such things again. At the same time, he believes this chapter of his life is closing. He is trying to take an objective view of what happened, to come to terms with it rather than allow it to be a lifelong burden. He is determined to do everything in his power to stop such abuses happening to anyone else.

He credits his sporting background with helping him survive. His training, discipline and resilience carried him through the worst. He was exchanged on 31 December 2022.

*Source: Based on an interview by Suspilne News Ivano-Frankivsk https://cv.suspilne.
media/articles/26545, 26 December 2023. YouTube video https://www.youtube.com/
watch?v=YlLaBOSe5vY*

More about Olexiy Anulya:

Olexiy Anulya has written a book in Russian about his experiences: 'Jingle
    Bellz' (2025). Discussed with Sergey Auslender on https://youtu.be/
    GUUseL6jlEM?si=7j87ctV_dAmHT8BZ, 1hr 26 mins into the interview. Can
    be ordered via Google Docs link on the YouTube page, short link here: http://
    bit.ly/3JEXfnv.
'All your teeth are in place? And can you show your nails?': Oleksiy Anulya
    from Chernihiv spoke with Russian prisoners of war'. Article in Suspilne,
    Chernihiv 24 April 2024, https://suspilne.media/chernihiv/730345-vsi-zubi-
    na-misci-a-nigti-mozete-pokazati-oleksij-anula-z-cernigova-pospilkuvavsa-z-
    vijskovopolonenimi-rosianami/
'Nine months in Russian captivity.' Article by Olha Samsonenko in TEXTY.ORG.
    UA 3 December 2023, https://texty.org.ua/articles/111246/nine-months-in-
    russian-captivity-oleksii-anulia-told-how-he-was-starving-eating-worms-and-a-
    live-mouse/

Unconquered. The story of Olexandr Didur, a Ukrainian Prisoner of War

There were over 5000 Ukrainian POWs in the early years of the war. This is the
story of one who spent nearly 15 months in Russian captivity.

Olexander Didur was born in 1991 in Oleshky, Kherson region. At the beginning of 18th century there was Oleshkivska Sich, a Cossack fortress, then in 1928
Oleshky was renamed Tsyrupinsk after one of the communists who carried out the
Holodomor policy in that region of Ukraine. In 2016 the town was given back its
historical name. At the moment Oleshky is under Russian occupation.

Olexander has served in the Ukrainian Army since 2015, at first on the
'Zaporizhzhia' submarine and then as a marine in Mariupol.

On 24 February 2022 Senior Sergeant Olexander Didur of the 36th Marine
Brigade was in Pavlopil, about 30.6 km (19 miles) from Mariupol. In the opening
days of the offensive the Russians did more than advance: they pummelled towns
and villages around Mariupol with every kind of shell they had. That was the situation across the region—the sky was streaked with a violent array of flashes as munitions arced overhead.

Although the 36th Brigade was nominally responsible for air defence, it lacked
the weaponry to protect the sky. Missiles soon began to strike the brigade itself, and
the unit received orders to withdraw. It took them several days to reach Mariupol;
the front was chaotic and it was often impossible to tell where Ukrainian units

ended and Russian forces began. Eventually they took up defensive positions around the Illich works at Azovstal—the plant divided into Illich and Azovmash—charged, as best they could, with protecting the skies despite the shortage of ammunition. They fought fiercely, and many fell in those battles; those who survived were later taken into Russian captivity. As more Russian forces poured into the city, Mariupol became encircled. In May, during the extraction, Olexander was captured.

Olexander had been wounded on 6 April 2022. On 12 April all those wounded were taken prisoner. Olexander sees this as the right decision because the 36th Marine Brigade did not want to surrender. They wanted to break through. Rumours circulated that the 36th Marine Brigade had relinquished the fight a month before the extraction—rumours that were entirely false. The brigade fought stubbornly and with courage; they did not want to surrender. Conditions were desperate: virtually no food, almost no ammunition, only scraps—5 mm, 47 mm and 62 mm rounds and a handful of grenades—yet they fought on to the last bullet and the last trench. Around 70% of the brigade fell in those battles.

Eventually commanders authorised the surrender of the wounded and of women who could not be carried on in combat, because there was nothing left to fight with and no practical way to evacuate them. A list was drawn up for those to be handed over, and the order was known to the military leadership. Mariupol was encircled, though some of our men still managed to break out.

That was how Olexander came to be wounded. The Russian 'orcs' closed in on their position and fierce, often hand-to-hand fighting followed. The marines were well trained, but sheer numbers made holding ground almost impossible. To conserve ammunition they would let the enemy approach until it was almost upon them—their rule was, 'If you can't see his face, don't fire.' Then a tank began to advance. Initially it fired from distance; seeing no counterattack, it crept ever closer until it reached the left flank of their position. Olexander ordered his men down into the bunker and remained in the post to watch the tank. One man disobeyed that order and stayed one floor below—a decision that, Olexander says, saved his life.

As the tank closed, Olexander radioed the sighting: 'I see the target—distance, direction,' and so on. The crew in the tank knew there were Ukrainian soldiers in the building but not precisely where. He saw the gun barrel swing towards them and then the flash. The shell exploded three metres away and tore into the wall behind him. He does not remember what happened next. Nothing, by rights, should have been left of him.

When surgeons later examined him they were stunned to find shell fragments in his head and left hand—injuries that would usually prove fatal. Three fingers on his right hand had been torn off, the bones of his left hand were shattered and his left eye was destroyed. He bled heavily. Olexander believes that, in that moment, a guardian angel put its arms around him and took the blow; it seemed to take the worst of it so that he lived. A comrade carried him to the bunker. The other marines called to him but, as he was unable to answer, they assumed he was dead. Perhaps a faint moan reached them; they then began to give him first aid.

He regained consciousness in captivity. He had been captured while unconscious and, when he came round, found two Chechen guards standing over him. He may have been delirious; they prodded to make sense of his words. One man tapped him lightly on the head with the butt of his rifle and asked, 'Do you know where you are? Do you know who you are?' The other muttered, 'Leave him—he's going to die.'

He was taken to Hospital No. 15 in Donetsk. Bedridden, bandaged and unable to stand, he was fed by fellow prisoners while guards watched and interrogations continued. Fortunately, Olexander was not subjected to torture there.

Once he could walk to the lavatory, Olexander was transferred to the 'Zone'—the prison camp system—at Olenivka in Donetsk region. Olenivka later became notorious after an incident in which many prisoners of war were killed; the Russians blamed the Ukrainian army, while others say the attack was organised by the Russians to present the appearance that Ukrainians were killing their own soldiers. Olexander was held in Barrack No. 6.

When the guards arrived for duty furious as rabid dogs, they would drag prisoners to the observation post and beat them for no reason at all, as if to punish the prisoners for bad news on the front—proof, in their eyes, that things were going well for Ukraine and badly for Russia. 'Don't raise your heads!' they barked. The Geneva Conventions were routinely ignored. Early on, the first POWs faced brutal interrogations and regular abuse; dogs were set on prisoners, and many men were beaten to death.

The prisoners could hear the sound of explosions somewhere beyond the Zone. And if somewhere near them the war was still going on it could mean just one thing: Ukraine was still alive. As for the terrorist act in Olenivka the question arises why the Russians did it. Olexander explains that first of all a separate barrack was prepared for the terrorist act. It used to be a workshop so the guards made prisoners from different barracks take away all the tools from that workshop and fix the floor, then bring in beds and mattresses. This preparation work took a couple of days. After that the barrack was locked and no one was allowed to enter it. No prisoners were working on that side of the Zone although it was considered to be a work camp and the inmates were taken there to do all kinds of jobs: to weed grass and other work. Then barracks 1, 2, 9 and 10 were visited by a group of guards with a list of names. These were the barracks where the POWs from the Azov Regiment were kept.

According to the lists, the Azov prisoners were placed in the newly prepared barrack—and almost that same night the explosion occurred. Those who later collected the remains testified that the blast came from inside, not outside. Everything was blown outwards, which suggests the explosive had been planted beneath the floor to give the appearance that Ukrainians were killing their own soldiers. Satellite evidence subsequently showed no strikes coming from Ukraine in that sector at the time in question.

The Russians were enraged, the prisoners say, because Ukrainians continued to live and fight while many Russians lacked even the basics. Olexander had been defending his land; he did not want his family taken from him. In captivity the men tried to help and support one another as best they could.

Olexander emerged from the fighting an invalid. He lost three fingers on his right hand, leaving only a thumb and little finger, yet astonishingly he taught himself to write and to type messages with those two digits—despite being told it would be impossible. His left arm was shattered by some ten shell fragments, two of which passed above his elbow into the shoulder. The shoulder partially healed, but the arm remained effectively useless throughout his captivity, with no medical aid beyond the field first aid given in the bunker (the medics there were trained to North Atlantic Treaty Organisation (NATO) standards).

During fifteen months of captivity he received no further medical treatment until the exchange. By then nerve atrophy had set in and the left arm's function could not be fully restored. Since his return he has undergone several operations and still requires more. His arm does not function properly, but Olexander refuses to give up—he remains determined that, against the odds, it will recover.

The Ukrainian state offered Olexander little help with rehabilitation. Disabled servicemen who defended the country receive only Hr700–800 (about $20) a month. While they do get hospital treatment covered by the state, they still need to feed their families, plan for the future and adapt to life with disabilities. In practice many turn to private clinics funded by volunteers, because the state shows little interest in their fate. Throughout his recovery Olexander was supported by the volunteer project 'The Heart of Azovstal.' Through them he and his family were provided with a free flat outside Kyiv—a lifeline for the family of four for which he can never be sufficiently grateful. The private clinic Adonis has helped with his rehabilitation.

While Olexander was fighting in Mariupol, his wife was in Mykolaiv, pregnant with their second child. At night the shelling forced her and their daughter to shelter in the bathtub; the next morning she was taken to the maternity unit, only for the bombardment to resume. She was led into a bunker and, despite needing a Caesarean, managed to give birth to a baby boy practically standing up—under fire.

Olexander now dreams of opening a rehabilitation centre for servicemen—especially those returning from Russian captivity or carrying war wounds. He wants it to offer not only medical help but also support in finding meaning, work and a stable life; to be a place that keeps in touch with people and makes sure they are coping. He wants to inspire others and believes that steady, step-by-step effort will bring success. That is also why he believes Ukraine will win this war.

Source: Interview by Yanina Sokolova, 30 November 2023. https://youtu.be/1zNyG55 NGBI?si=AYV3BTMkVQfa3CZr

Anatoliy Voloshyn, the Oldest Man in Russian Captivity

Anatoliy was the oldest man in Russian captivity at the age of 65. A native of Mariupol, he had worked at Azovstal as a bulldozer driver and later became a pastor. He and his wife had four children of their own and had adopted three more. When the full-scale Russian invasion began on 24 February 2022, Anatoliy thought that hostilities would end soon but despite that on 24 February he enrolled in a territorial defence unit and was issued with military equipment and weapons. He took the oath. As a pastor he had had to make the decision whether to take up arms. Later, in captivity, he was asked 'How could it be that you are a pastor and took up arms?' and his answer was 'This is between me and God. No one has the right to tell me what I can or cannot do. The invaders came to steal and kill and destroy and I came forward to defend my home.'

Anatoliy remembers how he and other territorial defence soldiers and servicemen were brought to Azovstal and he began to help the Azov defenders. He was able to make use of his experience as a bulldozer driver because at night they were digging trenches. They had to smash their headlights with hammers so that the light would not betray their location: enemy drones were flying above them and the Russians were firing from the sea and from the air. On 14 March Anatoliy's comrade-in-arms and Anatoliy himself came under mortar fire when a shell exploded under the bulldozer hood but luckily, Anatoliy's body armour saved him. A shell fragment entered under his ribs and another shell wounded his hand. He was operated on in a hospital near the Neptune Swimming Pool. The swimming pool was where pregnant women and children took refuge and it was attacked by the Russians on 16 March.

The day after his operation, Anatoliy lay in bed by the window when a shell struck. The glass exploded inward, showering him with shards, and a nurse cried: 'Whether you like it or not, you must get to the basement.' He had just been operated on and still had fresh stitches. Weak, cut and barefoot, he wrapped himself in a blanket and stepped across the broken glass to the shelter.

After that strike the wounded were moved to Azovstal. Anatoliy was treated in an underground hospital room. Russian air raids and shelling were constant; at one point the bunker canteen was hit and food had to be dug out from the rubble. They managed to salvage two tins of sardines for five people, then found oats and moistened them with drops of water. The defenders were remarkable—always scraping together water and supplies for the wounded. Some 300 people were crammed into that bunker hospital. There was barely enough water, food, light or air. It was, they said, true hell.

On 15 May the fighting finally stopped. For the first time Anatoliy could breathe fresh air; he rejoiced at the sight of green grass, even as the shell-scarred ruins of Azovstal smouldered around him. Over the following four days—on 17 May and the days after—more than three thousand Azov defenders left Azovstal as prisoners of war. They boarded buses bound for Olenivka. As soon as they arrived, all their possessions were taken from them.

Medical care was minimal. Food amounted to a ladleful of porridge, a thin sauerkraut soup (shchi—essentially water and sauerkraut) and one-sixteenth of a loaf of bread per meal, three times a day. Dinner was served at two in the morning. Hunger was constant; leaving the canteen you felt ravenous again, so to conserve energy Anatoliy would lie down and try to sleep. With up to 450 POWs crammed into a cell meant for 100, there were not enough beds; some men slept beneath the bunks. Conversation usually turned to food—how they used to cook, and for whom—because the tongue always returns to the sore tooth. News from the front was scarce.

About 900 Azov defenders were held there initially; after a short while they were separated from other prisoners and moved to a separate building. It was known that men with tattoos, especially Nordic runes, were singled out for particularly severe beatings, which seemed odd given that some Russian guards also bore rune tattoos.

Anatoliy spent three weeks in Olenivka. On 10 June the Russians read out a list of names and ordered those men to pack. He assumed he was being moved for an exchange, but the transport bypassed Donetsk, turning instead toward Makiivka, Vuhlehirsk and Debaltseve. When the convoy kept going beyond Debaltseve he realised they were headed for Russia.

They reached the Sverdlovsk penal colony and were met with blows from clubs. The guards were clearly angry and fearful of the POWs. About 200 Ukrainian prisoners were kept there; at first each received a quarter loaf of bread and half a plate of porridge. Anatoliy expected this to be a one-off, but in fact the meals there were relatively generous, and a daily routine settled in. From time to time the men were subjected to checks and interrogations.

Once Anatoliy was asked: 'What are you doing here, old man?'. He answered: 'I was defending my home.'

All Ukrainian POWs were called 'fascists' by the Russians and Anatoliy, because he wore glasses, was called 'the fascist intellectual.' This was a kind of praise and it kept him encouraged. All the prisoners had to do some work—some built beds in exchange for cigarettes. Those were the beds used for the prisoners. In the carpentry shop they also made one thousand coffins a month for Russian servicemen from wooden ammunition boxes.

Anatoliy read the Bible and tried to encourage his fellow prisoners by saying that they had a special mission there.

The prisoners were often forced to listen to Russian television, notably the propagandist Olga Skabeyeva. When she asked on air, 'How are things there? Is there any victory?' it sounded to the men like proof they were isolated and powerless. But when she reported that Biden or other European leaders were visiting Ukraine, or spoke about meetings such as Ramstein, the prisoners would quietly reassure one another: we are not alone—dozens of countries are supporting Ukraine—and that knowledge kept their spirits alive.

On 7 March 2023 a further prisoner exchange took place and 130 Ukrainian defenders returned home; Anatoliy was among them. Two weeks before the exchange the prisoners had been taken to the Russian headquarters and told they were being prepared for handover. Anatoliy's heart raced with hope, though he felt sorrow that many fellow POWs would remain behind. A week went by with no exchange and hope began to fade. Then one evening the Russians announced they would depart at 6 a.m.—and shortly afterwards announced the plan was off. Later that same night they took 28 men from Anatoliy's barrack and 50 from another, 78 in total, and brought them to the bathhouse to wash.

Showers were a rare luxury. Prisoners were usually permitted one wash a week, typically on Saturdays; fifty men would cram into the bathhouse under ten spouts of water. The flow was a trickle and each man had just five minutes. Over the months of his captivity Anatoliy estimated he had had only about forty baths in all.

After the shower the guards searched the prisoners' belongings, threatening that anyone found with a phone or even a scrap of paper would be excluded from the exchange. Fortunately Anatoliy managed to hide the telephone numbers of the wives of men who remained in captivity. The Russians then bound the prisoners' hands and blindfolded them with duct tape before herding them onto a bus. It was a long drive—perhaps to Taganrog—and then they were loaded onto a plane, seated shoulder to shoulder, hands still tied. It was stifling and there was no toilet. They were not given water so they would not need one.

The convoy stopped at the Sumy region border, and that was where the exchange took place. Anatoliy could not speak; there was a lump in his throat and tears in his eyes. He phoned his sons and told them he was home.

During his captivity he saw no human rights defenders or representatives of the International Committee of the Red Cross. After the exchange he received hospital treatment and psychological therapy. He had longed, in captivity, for apples, fresh fruit, vegetables and vitamins, and was grateful to have them again at home. He visited friends and army chaplains and decided that, after rehabilitation, he would return to the front to help the servicemen—he was already enrolled with the Mariupol chaplain's battalion. Anatoliy wants to be useful, active and helpful: 'Otherwise I will get old very soon,' he told his interviewer.

Source: Suspilne (https://bit.ly/3Yjk4jV), 17 May 2023.

Nazariy Gryntsevych from Vinnytsia. One of the Youngest AZOV Fighters

Nazariy had dreamed of joining the army from childhood, determined on a military career from the age of 14. He believed it was the most noble occupation for a man. When the Russian war started in Ukraine in 2014, Nazariy promised himself that if the war lasted till he was 18, he would join the army to defend his family, his land, and his country. In fact, Nazariy was 11 when Russia started the war in Ukraine. His patriotism and love of Ukraine started in childhood with the Ukrainian celebration of Vyshyvanka Day or the Day of Ukrainian Folk Tales. This is celebrated every year in Ukraine as a holiday designed to preserve traditional Ukrainian national clothing. A Vyshyvanka is an embroidered shirt or blouse, and symbolizes beauty, strength, and family.

Nazariy closely followed the Revolution of Dignity in 2014—the Maidan protests that began in Kyiv's Independence Square after President Yanukovych refused to sign an association and trade agreement with the European Union (EU) in favour of closer ties with Russia. He was too young to travel to Kyiv and join the demonstrations, but he watched the events intently and felt their impact.

When fighting broke out in the Donbas, Nazariy saw the soldiers returning from the battles for Donbas Airport. Many came back maimed; he understood—dimly, at that age—that their injuries were the price paid for independence. Their courage and sacrifice meant that he and his classmates could continue going to school, enjoy family life and live with a degree of peace. He could not grasp all the complexities of the conflict then, but he knew enough to be shaped by it.

Nazariy's first encounter with the Azov Regiment came at a football match when he was 14. He had gone to the stadium to support the local team, Nyva, and noticed that many of the fans from Vinnytsia and the surrounding region were serving in Azov and were passionate supporters of the unit. His curiosity grew: he began reading about them online, watching videos and studying patriotic ideas. It felt like a calling.

From 16 he trained seriously so he could join Azov. He understood that physical fitness, moral fibre and intellect all mattered. He read widely about military history and the Cossack fighters, and those studies helped him pass the interviews and the KMB training course for young recruits. One hundred and twenty men began the course; only about half completed it and were admitted—selection was strict and not based on popularity but on ability.

The KMB was a real school of endurance and professionalism. Training ran around the clock and included obstacle courses in full kit—body armour, helmet, a machine-gun and extra weights. It also taught the ethos of mutual support: if someone collapsed from exhaustion, the others would take plank or do press-ups until their comrade recovered and rejoined them. Recruits learned close-quarters fighting, first aid for themselves and wounded comrades, topography and combat tactics. Those basics were essential: skills to rely on in the field and the foundations of a professional soldier.

Nazariy achieved the top grade in tactical medicine during his KMB exams and decided to take a paramedic course—it would be his first formal medical training course. His only prior 'training' had been an episode from boyhood: out fishing with friends, one of them cut his leg and Nazariy stitched the wound using a fishing hook and line.

He first visited Mariupol shortly before his eighteenth birthday, in February. The railway station left no particular impression—just a small-town station much like those in his native Vinnytsia—so he went straight to the town centre: the Drama Theatre, the main street, and the water tower (which, he noted, resembled Vinnytsia's because it was built by the same architect). From a distance he glimpsed the vast Azovstal steelworks; he had no idea then of the role it would later play in his life. The main purpose of the trip, however, was practical: to submit his papers to the Azov Regiment. He returned to Vinnytsia and, on turning eighteen, was formally admitted to the KMB—the Course for Young Fighters—of the Azov Regiment.

Nazariy was first posted to the artillery division, where he trained for a month before joining the main KMB course. Azov maintained a special-operations capability, and artillery training there meant learning every aspect of gun work rather than a single narrowly defined task. As a result, each artilleryman could replace another: you might begin as a maintainer or a gunner, then move on to targeting, become second in command or even Master Gunner. That flexibility made personal development possible and kept the unit resilient. After a month in artillery, Nazariy returned to the KMB as a young fighter in the Azov Regiment.

Ukraine had been warned about a full-scale Russian invasion, but few believed it would happen. Back in the ninth grade, Nazariy told his classmates that the conflict in Donbas might escalate—Ukrainian independence had been won without a single drop of blood after the USSR's collapse, and that peace could come at a price. He understood, even then, that the war in Donbas was part of that price. He did not expect the widescale destruction and civilian suffering that followed, yet like his sworn brothers he was ready to fight the invaders at any time. Everyone who joined Azov knew what was expected: to accept any combat mission as an honour, because it meant your commander trusted you. It was a chance to show your skill, to cover your comrade's back and to defend your land.

Two months before the full-scale invasion, Nazariy's artillery unit was training in anti-amphibious defence. On 20 February they moved into position and slept under the tarpaulins of their KrAZ off-road truck. In the early hours of 24 February, at 04:45, a combat alert came over the radio. They fired up the KrAZ and made for their fighting posts, expecting an amphibious assault—enemy troops landing from ships on the shore, a kind of Normandy-style operation. Nazariy and his sworn brothers were ready for it.

What happened instead was different and far worse: the Russians advanced by road, coming through Kherson, Berdyansk and Melitopol. Nazariy's unit headed for Mariupol along the same route, as did other Azov detachments from nearby towns and villages. Everyone knew their orders; the commanders briefed them and the men prepared for whatever came next.

Nazariy stayed with his artillery unit until 15 May 2022. Between 10.00 and 14.00 one day they fired 217 rounds. Bear in mind that a Soviet-type gun risks the barrel itself failing after about 30 rounds—so that was a staggering number of shots. Then, from 15–18 March, their position came under direct assault. At first two aircraft launched missiles at them; by luck no one was killed or wounded and the guns survived. Later the Russians brought in 152 mm artillery, which put their guns out of action. Their commander then asked if they were ready to fight as infantry in the street battles; the men answered in unison, 'Yes.'

Nazariy was issued a Kalashnikov and assigned two young soldiers who had yet to finish KMB training. They soon discovered he carried a medical first-aid pack and that he was trained as a paramedic. Given the plan for his sector, he took up a position covering three buildings. As the sole paramedic for that sector, whenever he was not firing his Kalashnikov he would leave his post, instruct the other two soldiers on what to do, and rush to attend the wounded.

How Nazariy got his first wound

Nazariy's first wound came from a tank. After withdrawing from their initial position, they occupied a school shaped like the Ukrainian letter П. The fighting around there was ferocious: they'd already destroyed two enemy infantry groups when a Russian Tiger armoured vehicle reached Nazariy's sector and put their position out of action. They had only two man-portable anti-tank launchers—the crude 'Mookha' or 'fly'—and Nazariy knew the tank had to be stopped. He ran into the middle of the road, fired at the vehicle and struck it; smoke rose from the tank. With one Mookha and an RPG left, he and his sworn brother decided to fire together. 'It's probably a daft idea,' they said, 'but if you don't take risks you don't drink champagne.' Nazariy braced the Mookha while his comrade prepared the RPG.

Nazariy reached the corner of the school building from where he was meant to run out and fire, but at that instant the tank swung its barrel and fired. He was thrown by the blast, concussed, and left with bruised, perhaps fractured ribs. With electricity cut across Mariupol and no X-ray available at Azovstal, he still does not know the full extent of his injuries. Thrown back by the shock, he lost his hearing for some twenty minutes and was disoriented, yet his sworn brothers were at his side comforting him. They kept repeating, 'Grinka, Grinka, everything is OK—stay where you are.' (Grinka, a nickname meaning 'toast', had been given to him because he loved toast.) Almost automatically he drew his Makarov pistol and called, 'Let's go and take the Russians.' For those twenty minutes he lay recovering while his comrades continued to fight. When he came round he found himself in a basement and at that very second saw another tank entering their position. The vehicle rolled into the schoolyard but, unable to turn, it began to reverse straight towards the basement where he crouched. He grabbed grenades and hurled them under the treads, firing his Kalashnikov at the vehicle as he tried to halt its advance. The tank kept reversing and smashed into the building, forcing rubble and smoke into the yard. He remembered the faces of the men who had helped him, their eyes hard and kind; the smell of burning diesel and cordite filled the air, mingled with dust and the copper tang of blood. He felt gratitude and a stubborn, numbed disbelief that he was still alive; in that awful calm he vowed to keep fighting for them all for his family too. By radio he told his sworn brother: 'The tank is backing on me; I might be 200 (military jargon for dead)—but thank you for serving with me.' His comrade replied: 'Grinka, stay calm. I'll think of something.' Nazariy threw more grenades under the tank while his comrade ran up to the third floor, set up his Mookha and fired.

They knocked out the PKT, the tank's machine-gun, and the vehicle began to billow smoke. For a moment they thought a few grenades would finish it and put another Russian tank out of action. To their surprise it limped away. The fighting continued through the day until nightfall; the Russians, realising they could not take the position that day, eased off. That evening blood trickled from Nazariy's ears and he felt violently sick—he was in very poor shape.

Next morning the battles resumed with even greater ferocity. Nazariy needed evacuating, but the corridor was swept by mortars. While tending and evacuating the wounded he had an idea where the checkpoint should be, although he was far from fully conscious. He changed into civilian clothes, tucked his pistol into his pocket and began to make his way toward where he thought the lifeguard point lay. Somewhere along the route he collapsed. Fortunately his sworn brothers found him and dragged him to the evacuation point. That was how he reached the Azovstal Zhalizyak hospital—he could not recall the exact date, only that it was between about 29 March and 1 April.

When Nazariy reached the hospital his heart ached at the sight of his brothers lying in squalid, insanitary conditions—missing arms, missing legs, empty eye sockets, shrapnel and bullet wounds, carries of severe amputations. These were the men he had trained and laughed with; seeing them like that made him ache to help. He lost consciousness and only came round the following morning.

On waking he spoke to some of the wounded and learned how badly they had been hurt. He realised his own injuries were less severe than many of theirs and felt he had to return to the fight. He asked his commander for orders and, because he was still weak, was given duties he could manage from the bunker: dressing wounds, fetching food, visiting bunkers where civilians were sheltering. His comrades accepted their fate as soldiers—they knew what might happen—but the civilians were another matter entirely.

Seeing women and children sleeping under bombardment, with nothing to eat or drink, was heartbreaking for Nazariy. He thought of his own sister and brother at home. He and his sworn brothers did everything they could to find food, nappies or small comforts. Nazariy used a tablet to download games for the children—he used to like 'Angry Birds' himself—and they even found two kittens to give to youngsters so they would have something to play with.

Nazariy felt they were fighting and shedding blood for the future of those people; they would do anything for them. Fortunately, a green corridor was negotiated and the civilians were evacuated from Azovstal. The soldiers cheered for them, relieved that those civilians no longer had to endure the same conditions. After the evacuations the Russians intensified their air bombardment of the Azovstal complex, dropping high-explosive bombs.

When Nazariy had recovered enough—though he was far from fully healed—he joined an anti-tank group tasked with destroying enemy vehicles. They fought effectively, but then the Russians began to rain high-explosive aerial bombs on them. One bunker was pulverised and 64 soldiers were killed under the rubble; shortly afterwards another blast collapsed a second bunker, killing 56 more. It was staggeringly senseless—in a single minute you could lose 64 friends: someone's children, husbands, brothers, sons.

In those moments the men thought of their comrades in the Zhalizyak hospital, many in a desperately bad way, and of how many had already suffered under bombardment. Bitterly, they joked that it would have been easier if the Russians had killed them at their home bases; if the assault had come from the sea at the outset, none of this would have happened. Still, the Azov soldiers did not lose hope. There were even fevered plans to don civilian clothes and try to strike back using undercover operations. Every man knew what he was fighting for; they wore the Azov chevron with pride and were prepared to fight to the last.

How Nazariy was wounded for the second time

Nazariy rejoined the anti-tank group. On 15 April came the so-called crossing—the move from the right bank of the Kalmius River, to the Azovstal works. Russian forces were massive, while Azov fighters were split between the right bank and the left bank at Azovstal, which made it extremely hard to consolidate, to supply colleagues with food and ammunition, or to evacuate the wounded. For that reason the regimental command decided to form one strong 'fist': to concentrate all Azov personnel at Azovstal, a complex bordered by water on three sides and therefore easier to defend, with bunkers to shelter the wounded. United, they would be stronger. The order was to cross to Azovstal.

Nazariy remembered that night clearly. He was told to pack his rucksack: soldiers would be crossing the river and his team must cover and assist them. Of course he was ready. His group took six stretchers. The hangars at Azovstal could be reached by water; the first men to cross went on foot. It was April—cold and hard going—but they made the move.

The soldiers set out in full kit, machine-guns slung, and had to swim the river carrying their wounded. Enemy fire was relentless and terrifying. When Nazariy reached Azovstal he realised the column was being hammered with everything the Russians had: Grad rocket salvos, 152mm rounds and swarms of reconnaissance and attack drones that made the aiming brutally precise. They were not only shooting at the crossing but at the steelworks itself—the sky seemed to be on fire.

Hundreds of Azov fighters were hit; Nazariy and his team hauled those who could not reach the bank out of the water and onto stretchers. If he could, he administered first aid; if not, he evacuated them to the medical transport that would take the wounded into the Azovstal complex. When the crossing finally ended the defenders agreed it had been the worst day of their lives—yet they also knew it was not the end; the fight would go on.

Nazariy was wounded again on 16–17 March while he and his group were returning to their shelter after a day's mission. They were approaching the bunker when Russian 152 mm guns began firing at the blast furnaces. One shell landed 200–300 metres away, then a second, and the third struck about ten metres from Nazariy, lifting him into the air.

He checked his arms and legs—they seemed intact—then poked at his teeth with his tongue. Mercifully none had been knocked out, but blood was running down his face. Practically blind, he staggered into the bunker, looked at his phone and realised his maxillary sinus and nose were broken. A cigarette was handed to him; when he lit it, smoke puffed from his sinus.

With only chlorhexidine available, he cleaned the wound and they managed to extract a metal fragment. Tanya, one of the nurses, dressed it with gauze. He declined to go to hospital—there were men in far worse condition who needed urgent care, and getting there would have been difficult. The left side of his face lost all sensation and remains numb to this day; he remembers feeling no pain there, only swelling. The bony palate at the roof of his mouth was also fractured.

Nazariy had his face bandaged and, the next morning, he and his group were back in the fighting. The battles grew heavier each day as the Russians pushed into the Azov plant itself; fierce close-quarters fighting broke out inside the works and the casualty lists swelled. Many Azov defenders were killed.

He can only speak for himself and his sworn brothers, but all of them fought for the same thing—an independent Ukraine. They paid with their lives; they were heroes, tigers in battle, unafraid to face a stronger, treacherous foe. Nazariy wants every Ukrainian to remember that and to tell their children and grandchildren about the courage of the Azov defenders. He believes all Ukrainians should be proud: these men helped give others the chance to sit with a cup of coffee, enjoy family life, and live in freedom.

Nazariy tried to contact his family once a day—usually no more than a five-minute call. He'd tell his mum that everything was fine, that he was sitting with his mates, chatting and relaxing. In truth, there were only three or four Starlink terminals for the whole of Azovstal, so if you got a turn online the priority was simple: reassure your family that you were alive and well. There wasn't time to follow events beyond the plant; Nazariy didn't read the news.

As a serviceman he understood the grim reality of the situation: it was an almost impossible military problem and there would be no easy way out. All the same, they resolved to fight to the end. Early in the siege they had even watched footage of Kharkiv conscripts destroying tanks with shoulder-fired RPGs—a reminder of what courage and improvisation could achieve.

They had seen footage of men from the Kyiv region taking on tanks with Javelins. Those videos inspired Nazariy and his sworn brothers—proof that the whole of Ukraine was standing up to the invaders. Ukraine had not surrendered, and they were determined to do their part in Mariupol. Nazariy felt they needed to fight in a way that would make the Russians fear them—and, in fact, the defenders did inspire that fear.

The Azovstal command began recording short reports. Nazariy's friend Kalyna described the reality inside the plant and in the hospital: the desperate shortages of food and water. These were not tales for effect—they were true. Nazariy and four friends shared a single 1.5-litre bottle of water a day; in the last week before capture they had to split a plastic cup of porridge between five men, with only hard tack to supplement it. Imagine how exhausted they were, physically and morally. Think of the badly wounded—those with amputated limbs or abdominal injuries—and how impossible rehabilitation seemed without food, medicine or even a moment's proper sleep beneath the unending bombardment.

Then, after returning from a mission, their commander told them they would be evacuated—straight into captivity. Nazariy feared being a prisoner of war; he knew the word carried its own horrors. But when he learned his commander Redis and the other leaders would be leaving alongside the rank and file, he realised the ordeal might be harder for those commanders than for a simple soldier like him. Why, he asked himself, should he be more afraid? He promised his mother he would come back.

Russian Captivity

The Azov defenders began leaving the plant, and in the first two days they evacuated the wounded—everyone from the Zhalizyak hospital, those with amputations and the seriously injured. Nazariy himself was taken into Russian captivity on 18 May 2022. He was first held in Olenivka for two months (Olenivka is the site where, later, Azov prisoners were blown up in one of the barracks), then moved to the Donetsk prosecutor's office, the Donetsk military court and finally the Donetsk pre-trial detention centre.

Throughout his captivity the fragment of shell remained lodged in his face; despite telling his captors that metal was embedded there and that he had lost sensation on that side, he received no medical treatment. Only after the exchange, back in Ukraine, was he operated on—the metal was removed and his nose was straightened.

During his captivity the Russians recorded a long interview with Nazariy—part of it is on the internet. He still remembers some of the questions. One interviewer asked: 'Have you seen Ukrainian soldiers abusing Russian prisoners?' Nazariy replied, 'No. I haven't seen anything like that—and where could I have seen it? We Ukrainians have honour. I did see a video in which the Kadyrovtsi boasted that they would kill us all.'

Another question was, 'What is your view of President Zelensky?' Nazariy answered simply: 'He is the commander-in-chief and he is doing everything to win this war.' The interviewer snapped back, 'Oh, it's not a war—it's a special military operation.' Nazariy shot back: 'Perhaps it is a 'special military operation' for you, the Russians, but for me this has been a war since 2014.' When they accused him of 'bombing Donbas for eight years,' he retorted, 'You Russians boast you destroyed Mariupol in two months—imagine what eight years of bombardment would do to Donbas.'

They also asked, 'Why would someone as young as you join the Azov Regiment?'

Whatever facts Nazariy gave, the Russians tried to twist them to suit their propaganda. They aired an extract of the interview framed by the question, 'Would you follow the orders of your commander?' Nazariy replied: 'Yes. If there had been such an order, I would have held my position to the last. I am a serviceman and I trust my commanders completely. I am ready to go into my last battle; if that battle had to be in Mariupol, I would not spare my blood. I would gladly shed my blood for Mariupol, for my country, for my loved ones and relatives, for my friends.'

The Russians did not like those answers, and after the interview they turned on him. Nazariy says he would like the whole interview to be seen—not the edited extracts—because it reveals the essence of the 'Russkiy Mir' propaganda he encountered and how they distort the truth.

How Nazariy was exchanged from Russian captivity

Until the very end Nazariy could not bring himself to believe he would be exchanged. The procedure was brutal: sacks over their heads and tape across their eyes. He managed, however, to slip the tape enough to peep and see where they were being taken. He watched the road out of Donetsk, then Taganrog, until they reached an airfield where an IL-76 touched down and the prisoners were ushered on board.

Nazariy sat close to the flight mechanic and watched the instruments, noting the time and the altitude as the aircraft climbed. The plane touched down in Moscow at 10:45 and the crew changed, then they took off again. He asked the mechanic, 'I'm nineteen—where are we going?' The man answered, 'We're in Moscow now. We're off to Belarus.'

A tiny spark of hope flared—perhaps this really would be an exchange. When the aircraft touched down in Belarus they took the ropes off their hands and herded them onto a coach with comfortable seats. The guards continued to swear and to exert psychological pressure, but when they crossed the border the hoods were removed and the tape taken from their eyes. The prisoners saw Ukrainian flags, a large poster reading 'Welcome to Ukraine' and cars with Ukrainian plates.

For about a week Nazariy still could not quite believe it. Even when he hugged his mother it felt unreal: the impossible fact that he was free of Russian captivity. That disbelief lingers—he still thinks constantly of those who remain behind. He knows how hard it is to survive a winter in captivity. Exchanged on 21 September 2023, Nazariy wishes all his comrades were home with him; he believes they are the finest sons of Ukraine and deserve to be returned. He hopes the government will do everything in its power to bring every Ukrainian POW back.

Nazariy dreamed of a peaceful life: of starting a family, taking his daughter to school and his son to nursery, and coming home in the evening to his wife cooking cutlets. Yet he knew the war was not over and that, for now, everyone had to defend their Fatherland. He believed firmly in Ukraine's eventual victory and was determined to play his part in rebuilding the country. 'Every Ukrainian should be proud to be Ukrainian,' he would say, and ask what each of us could do for our nation. To him, Ukraine was the best country in the world.

After rehabilitation Nazariy returned to the front. On 7 May 2024 he was killed in action. Glory to a hero.

*   *   *

Notes

Sworn brother: the Ukrainian tradition of brotherhood dates back to the time of the Scythians. There is even a Ukrainian proverb saying: 'Friendship and brotherhood are more precious than any treasure.' There was a special ceremony in the Ukrainian Cossack army when men about to become sworn brothers were bound by ties of friendship swearing loyalty to each other. They would also exchange their crosses and would present horses and weapons to each other. When one of them was captured (for example by the Turks and made to work hard in captivity) his sworn brother would come and exchange himself for his sworn brother. This phenomenon of sworn brothers made the Cossack army invincible. The same tradition was started in the Azov regiment.

This story is based on an interview with Nazariy after he was freed from Russian captivity. Source: LB Live (lb.ua). Interview on 6 December 2022. YouTube https:// youtu.be/js2PeqQvrac?si=i5Bijxu9Fn_0rMfO.

Maryana Chechelyuk, a 24 year old National Police Service investigator

Maryana Chechelyuk is from Mariupol. She spent two years and two months in Russian captivity.

Among the 75 POWs exchanged on 31 May 2024 were five women—four civilians and one servicewoman. It was the 52nd exchange; by that date a total of 3,135 Ukrainian POWs had been returned. Roughly one third were wounded or seriously injured and all required medical treatment and rehabilitation; many had lost more than 20 kg. One soldier from that exchange had suffered a stroke in captivity and would at last be able to receive professional care.

Prisoner transfers usually involved not only buses but several ambulances to carry the wounded. Not one person released from Russian custody had seen a representative of the Red Cross while interned. Women prisoners suffered in much the same way as men: their treatment and the tortures they endured were, tragically, comparable.

After the full-scale invasion began, Maryana and her younger sister sheltered from missile strikes at the Azovstal plant and tried to leave Mariupol through a 'green corridor.' At a Russian filtration camp, however, the occupiers discovered that Maryana had served with the National Police. She was arrested and sent to the Donetsk SIZO.

Over the years of her captivity she was held in some of the most notorious camps used for Ukrainian prisoners: Olenivka colony and the prisons in Taganrog and Mariupol. The Russians tried to turn her to their side, alternating promises of high pay in Russia with a range of threats, but their efforts failed.

Maryana endured repeated torture: she was starved, beaten and subjected to both physical and psychological abuse. Her health deteriorated rapidly. A severe cold and angina developed into chronic bronchitis. She was often kept in damp dungeons infested with rats and mice, and lost a great deal of weight; her hair thinned and her menstrual cycle stopped altogether. Letters her mother sent never reached her, so she had no idea what had become of her family or where they were.

On several occasions she was summoned for prisoner exchanges, only to be pulled back at the last moment. Each time the Russians told her it was because the Ukrainian side had refused the swap.

Although Maryana was a civilian who did not take part in combat, she was detained and treated as a prisoner of war, and only later released in a POW exchange. Under the Geneva Conventions she would not normally fall into the category of combatant and should not have been held as a POW.

Negotiating exchanges has been extremely difficult because Russia does not comply with the Geneva framework. The Ukrainian authorities therefore insist on two organising principles when negotiating swaps. First, priority should be given to the seriously wounded, then to women, and then to everyone else. Second, exchanges should also take account of how long people have been held, giving precedence to those detained the longest.

The Russians refuse to accept this logic and seem to apply their own 'Russian logic' instead. They may say they will consider Ukraine's principles for exchanges, but in practice they produce their own lists of POWs using their own criteria and then offer, blandly, 'If you want, we can exchange those.' Of course Ukraine agrees— its priority is to bring everyone home—but Kyiv never forgets who it is negotiating with. Russia treats prisoner exchanges with treachery and bad faith: it will change the terms, substitute names, or cancel an exchange at the last minute. You can never be sure an agreed swap will actually happen.

Source: TSN (https://bit.ly/3YiF0HX), 4 June 2024

Some shorter stories: Andriy Stepanov, Yuriy Gulchuk and Olexiy Ryzhnenko

Andriy Stepanov

'Because I was tortured with electric shock on my neck after having a shower my heart stopped beating. Luckily, their doctors managed to revive me. I assume that having accidents in their prisons is not a desirable thing. Occasionally they have inspections and the data has to be good'.

Actually, his heart stopped twice.

Source: www.youtube.com/shorts/tp74cU60ZZA, from Suspilne Chernivtsi (www. youtube.com/@SuspilneChernivtsi). 24 September 2024

Full interview on www.youtube.com/watch?v=Wb9HaJ3dYU8

Yuriy Gulchuk

Twenty-two-year-old marine Yuriy Hulchuk was held in Russian captivity from April 2022 until 14 September 2024. Repeated beatings and electric shocks left his legs numb and robbed him, for a time, of speech and sensation.

When he was returned, he looked at his mother with an empty stare, as if looking through her; he showed no emotion and did not recognise her until the third day back in Ukraine. Doctors were initially pessimistic, but gradually Yuriy began to speak again—with a slight lisp—and has even made attempts to stand and walk. For now his simplest wish is achingly small: to be able to step outside for a smoke— but walking on his own.

His first words after regaining his speech were: 'Why so much pain? Why so many lies? Why are people so cruel to each other?'

Source: www.youtube.com/watch?v=qxdNRucUa-A. September 2024

Olexiy Ryzhnenko

Olexiy Ryzhynenko, a border guard from Kherson region, spent 28 months in Russian captivity. 'There are moments I don't even want to talk about,' he says. 'They did terrible things. They fed us only once a day—boiling water poured over half an onion ring in a disposable plate. I began to lose weight very fast. When I came home I weighed 65 kg compared with 95 kg before captivity. Over two-and-a-half years I was given apples, onion or garlic only a few times.'

He remembers the moment he saw the sign for home. 'I can't describe how I felt when I saw 'Welcome to Ukraine'. I wanted to cry and shout.'

Source: www.youtube.com/shorts/oc4wK4xQTpI, 16 September 2024

Section Introduction: Occupation

The Russian occupation of Crimea and the Donbas regions of Donetsk and Luhansk began in the spring of 2014, long before the Russian full-scale invasion of Ukraine in February 2022. Kyiv had been immersed in the 'EuroMaidan' protests since November 2013, as thousands of protesters gathered in its main square, the Maidan, when President Yanukovych refused to sign a cooperation agreement with the EU. The protests gathered force and were met with violence by the Berkut riot police. Over 100 protesters and 13 police officers were killed and many more wounded. Eventually Yanukovych was ousted on 22 February 2014, fleeing to Russia, and the country returned to the 2004 Constitution in what became known as the Revolution of Dignity.

In the confusion of the days that followed—including protests against the Revolution of Dignity in parts of southern and eastern Ukraine, Russia began its occupation, all the time masking its involvement with disinformation and even denial.

The annexation of the Autonomous Republic of Crimea began only a week later, on 27 February, with the appearance of armed men in unmarked military fatigues, known as 'little green men' by the locals but understood by everyone to be Russian special forces despite Russia's denials. They began to take over strategic areas. By March Putin had admitted involvement, the invaders took over the Crimean parliament, conducted a rushed referendum and declared 'Crimea is Ours' (the slogan 'Krym Nash' became very popular in Russia).

When Russia moved into the Donbas regions of Donetsk and Luhansk in April the strategy was similar. Its soldiers were said to be 'separatists', by implication all disgruntled locals, or even 'tourists' from Russia who had picked up camouflage outfits in some sort of sports shop and had come to support the separatists. There were hastily arranged referendums, as in Crimea, and similarly they were not recognised by Ukraine or the democratic West. Donetsk and Luhansk were declared Russian Republics, formally recognised by Russia in 2022, three days before the launch of the full-scale invasion. Over time 'Russification' has moved on from mandatory Russian passports and the Russian language to military exercises for young people, even those in nursery schools—mirroring practice in Russia.

The Ukrainian army has been engaged in the Donbas since 2014 and this was the real beginning of the Russo-Ukrainian war. In 2022, having failed to occupy

Kyiv and Kharkiv in the early months of the full-scale invasion, Russia fell back on its base in Donbas and has been gradually increasing its hold on eastern Ukraine since then while continuing to launch missile attacks across the rest of the country from Crimea and Russia itself. In addition to annexing Crimea Russia has declared the Donetsk and Luhansk regions (oblasts) to be Russian republics and claims the Kherson and Zaporizhzhia regions too—although much of that territory including the administrative centres, the cities of Kherson and Zaporizhzhia, remains under Ukrainian control.

The stories in this section show the persecution of citizens from the early days of Russian occupation for any, or even no, divergence from the new rules. Including non-political and (as is common in the east) Russian-speaking citizens, men and women, old and young. We start with a short summary of the conditions in the occupied territories based mainly on information from refugees now in the UK.

Life in the Occupied Territories of Ukraine

Around 20% of Ukraine's territory is currently under Russian occupation. What is life like there? Here are some facts from the occupied towns on the Sea of Azov—Mariupol, Melitopol and Berdyansk—in Zaporizhzhia region, parts of which remain under Ukrainian control.

A village about 45 km from Mariupol is home to the sister of a refugee now living in the UK. She could not leave because their mother is an 80-year-old who needs care; their lives remain under constant threat.

At first the family refused to swap their Ukrainian passports for Russian ones. To push people into accepting Russian citizenship, the occupiers offered a one-off payment of 140,000 roubles (just over £1,000) to early applicants. The two women still resisted, but once their Ukrainian funds ran out they found they could not access pensions or even buy bread without a Russian passport and roubles. Faced with the choice between starving and accepting a Russian document, and needing medication for their elderly mother, they felt forced to comply. Because they delayed, however, the occupiers later marked them as 'unreliable'—their home is frequently searched and turned upside down.

*   *   *

When the Russians held their so-called elections, armed soldiers went house to house with ballot boxes. People were effectively forced to vote under constant surveillance—one wrong move felt like it could be fatal.

Electricity is often cut; locals say the pylons from Mariupol to neighbouring towns have been felled.

Above all, the psychological toll is immense. No one knows whom they can trust: neighbours may report you to the occupiers, phones and lines are often bugged, and contact with the outside world is severely limited. People live in a state of isolation and fear, while Russian television insists Ukraine does not exist. There have been appalling incidents: once a Russian soldier attempted to rape a girl in broad daylight; by sheer luck the community managed to save her.

Russian occupation is especially harsh for people who run businesses, notably farmers. Those who refuse to swap Ukrainian passports for Russian ones risk having their agricultural machinery seized; the occupiers then lease that equipment to so-called 'reliable' farmers who hold Russian documents. Crops and bank accounts are also confiscated.

Owners of comfortable homes fare little better: houses are commandeered for soldiers. In one village a couple who ran a shop had their business, their savings and their house taken—the occupiers permitted the wife to take only a few personal items.

The brother of a refugee now living in the UK comes from a village about 40 km from Mariupol. He was a respected doctor and a disabled pensioner who had just finished re-decorating his home before the war. The Russians confiscated the house. When he protested, saying 'You should all be in The Hague,' he was arrested. During his interrogation they offered him the chance to collaborate; he refused and luckily was released.

When the doctor's wife stepped into a shop and said, 'Glory to Ukraine,' a Russian soldier struck her on the head with the butt of his rifle. Fortunately her skull was not fractured, but she suffered a concussion and a bruised face. The family's misfortune did not end there: the house of the doctor's mother-in-law—a large two-storey home in the village centre—was seized and requisitioned for officers. One day soldiers simply told her, 'Tomorrow we will move into your house.'

The doctor eventually heard of a so-called green corridor organised nearby and managed, with help, to reach Ukrainian-held Zaporizhzhia. Even so, the journey was perilous: the convoy passed through numerous Russian checkpoints where guards demanded bribes and would not allow passage without payment. The Red Cross vehicle was at the rear of the column and, constrained by its mandate, was unable to intervene to pay those bribes needed to guarantee safe passage. Only through sheer luck and persistence did the doctor and his family make it to safety.

The doctor's friend Petro tried to flee to Rostov or Taganrog with his wife and two children by car. Because they owned a nice vehicle the Russians confiscated it and sent Petro to prison. His wife did everything she could to secure his release: she contacted relatives who pooled money to pay a large bribe. The payoff was so substantial that the jailers ordered Petro to leave Russian territory within 36 hours. With the help of friends he ultimately managed to get out of Russia and on to safety in Europe.

In occupied Melitopol around half the population refused to swap Ukrainian passports for Russian ones. To identify those who had resisted, the occupiers carried out a population census. By then Melitopol had been under occupation for nearly two years and the authorities were pressing ahead with a programme of Russification they hoped to complete by 1 January 2024. In their view, lacking a Russian passport meant you were on their territory illegally, so they subjected people to interviews designed to force them to surrender their Ukrainian documents.

Refusing a Russian passport has severe practical consequences. Without one you cannot register property, so you cannot be recognised as the owner of your flat or house—and, as a result, you may be denied electricity. You cannot sign contracts for internet and other services; you cannot register or legally drive a car without a Russian driving licence; and your access to pensions and benefits is effectively blocked. In short, the refusal to accept a Russian passport can mean being stripped of basic civil rights and livelihoods.

Moreover, anyone without a Russian passport cannot register with a medical clinic or access routine healthcare.

Worse still, lack of a Russian passport carries the threat of deportation. Until late 2022 deportations were typically carried out at the last Russian checkpoint in Vasylivka; since then the destination and mechanics of deportation have become increasingly opaque.

The occupiers are also pursuing a policy of demographic substitution. Leaflets offering 'attractive' jobs across the Russian Federation are distributed throughout Melitopol, encouraging residents to leave the temporarily occupied city so their places can be filled by newcomers from Russia—a tactic reminiscent of Soviet-era population transfers in Crimea and elsewhere.

Mobilisation has stepped up since the start of 2024. Russia has opened five new recruitment offices in Zaporizhzhia region, headed by retired officers from the Russian armed forces. Their job is to identify men of conscription age, subject them to a medical check and give them two or three days' basic military training—after which they are deemed fit for service. Some residents of Melitopol have already been drafted; unsure whether they can trust these men with weapons, the occupiers have largely used them to build fortifications on the frontline.

Melitopol's pre-war population was about 150,000; roughly 70,000 now remain under occupation, and some 35,000 of those have refused Russian passports. Nevertheless, Moscow is trying to manufacture an image of unanimous support in the occupied territories—a narrative it pushes hard as elections approach. Officials in Melitopol were pressured to collect signatures that were then sent to Moscow. The Kremlin presents these figures to the Russian public as proof that the local population backs the 'liberation', making it easier to argue that Russians need not fear fighting on the Ukrainian front because the locals supposedly support them. In reality, the occupiers are intensifying mobilisation in the territories precisely because they cannot rely on genuine consent.

The Russians have been trying to build a new railway to link Mariupol and Melitopol. Because the line would run close to the Zaporizhzhia front, they planned to route it along the Sea of Azov coast, but resistance activity has repeatedly frustrated them. Partisans have already destroyed a newly built Melitopol bridge, preventing the railway from becoming operational—a bridge Moscow apparently considered important in case its Crimean bridge ever came under Ukrainian attack.

Meanwhile the occupiers rely on highways to move lorries, troops, ammunition and materials for fortifications. They cloak their vehicles and prepare defensive positions, but the resistance is active: partisans have identified around 1,500 collaborators whose names, it is said, will be presented for trial when Ukraine reasserts control.

Between Mariupol and Melitopol lies Berdyansk, where Colony No. 77 has become, in survivors' words, an Auschwitz of the 21st century. A notorious torture complex in Zaporizhzhia region, popularly called 'the Basement,' it reportedly contains the largest number of Russian interrogation cells. Since March 2022 thousands of Ukrainians are said to have been processed there—only a few have emerged; the fate of many remains unknown. People are seized on suspicion of links to the Ukrainian armed forces or of passing information to them. Even photographs on a mobile phone can be used as a pretext for arrest: images found online or in a gallery—for example, a capsized Russian vessel in a nearby port—may be taken as evidence that the owner is a fire-support officer, and that person can be sent to 'the Basement.'

These accounts from occupied Zaporizhzhia are not unique to that region—they reflect patterns seen across all territories under Russian control since 2014.

One of the cruellest and least-discussed aspects of the occupation is the systematic abduction of Ukrainian civilians, including, by Ukrainian government estimates, at least some 20,000 children. An early example surfaced on 10 January 2024, when Belarusian state television in Mogilev ('Belarus 4. Mogilev') reported that 35 children had arrived from the town of Antratsyt in Luhansk region (occupied since 2014) to be looked after by the Ministry of Emergency Situations. In the broadcast the children wore tracksuits with Russian flags on the sleeves.

In addition, more than 1,500 adults are reported to have been seized in recently occupied areas on accusations of 'cooperating with the Ukrainian underground.' Repressive measures target civilians who show public dissent, and Russian special-forces units continue actively to hunt for partisans.

The woman who was tied to a pole

The events in this story took place in Donetsk in August 2014, long before the Russian invasion of Ukraine in February 2022 which led to all-out war. At that time Iryna Dovhan ran a beauty salon in Yasynuvata, a small town about 13 miles from Donetsk. She also volunteered, collecting donated items such as food, medicines and clothing and delivering them to Ukrainian soldiers nearby. The Vostok Battalion was a Russian militant group operating in Donbas, later becoming an official part of the Russian Armed Forces. They accused Iryna of spying for Ukraine and informing the soldiers of Russian troop movements, accusations she firmly denied. They wanted to make an example of her. The story also mentions Ossetian and Buryat soldiers—the Russian forces also included groups from Chechnya.

*   *   *

In occupied Donetsk, volunteer Iryna Dovhan endured a brutal, degrading ordeal in August 2014. Militants tied her to a pole and wrapped her in a Ukrainian flag. Forced to hold a placard reading 'Child-killer and Special Forces agent', she was exposed to a medieval spectacle of cruelty. Passers-by kicked her, spat at her and hurled insults. At one point a man in a white shirt with a badge and a large camera walked by; shortly afterwards two women stopped, stood in front of her and, with no hesitation, began to beat her while the cameraman filmed the savage attack.

The photograph he took eventually reached The New York Times—and, without exaggeration, that single image saved Iryna's life. After the public humiliation she was dragged back to the Vostok Battalion headquarters, where her abuse continued. This time the violence came from men: large, athletic figures who slapped and kicked her in the chest and ribs. She could not sleep that night; her whole body ached, and she could not even lie on the floor without suffering terrible pain.

Late the following evening an investigator crouched beside her, blew cigarette smoke in her face and said: 'Madam, you have become an internet star.' For a moment hope sparked in Iryna—she remembered the man in the white shirt with the large camera. Could he save her?

But the brutality continued: she was beaten again, humiliated and threatened with rape. When they returned that night she believed they were going to execute her. She clung to the floor and the walls with her fingernails, struggling to stop them dragging her from the cell.

In the end they did not take her to be killed but to a meeting attended by soldiers and journalists—all because of that photograph at the pole. The image, which captured the moment of public beating, travelled around the world and became a haunting symbol of the war in Donetsk. Had an American journalist not happened to pass by, documented the scene and published the pictures, it is likely Iryna would have been killed.

Before her release, the commander of the Vostok Battalion, Oleksander Khodokovsky, addressed journalists, calling Iryna's arrest a mistake and insisting that Vostok did not persecute dissidents. She was then compelled to sign a statement declaring she had no complaints, on pain of being prevented from leaving. American journalists helped secure her exit from Donetsk.

She has not returned to her beloved town, her cherished garden or her cosy home. Initially she went to Mariupol, which remained under Ukrainian control at the time, where her husband and daughter were caring for an elderly relative. From there the family relocated to Kyiv.

*   *   *

Iryna Dovhan had been detained, beaten, tortured and threatened with execution for her pro-Ukrainian stance. A few weeks after her release she was invited to address the UN Human Rights Council. She had so much to say but was allotted only two minutes, so she concentrated on the essentials: she described the abuses she had suffered in captivity and declared plainly that her torturers were sponsored by Russia. After her two-minute address she broke down in tears in the restroom—she had tried so hard to tell everything within that tiny slot of time.

Following her UN appearance, Iryna travelled to Switzerland hoping her account would shock the world into action. Again she was given only two minutes, yet the next day her testimony was carried widely in the international press—it had not been in vain; the world had heard her. Later she testified in Brussels at a preliminary tribunal hearing into war crimes committed by Russian forces in eastern Ukraine in 2014. Iryna was prepared to give the court full detail about her torture and humiliation—she believes it is vital that the world learns the truth and recognises Russia as an aggressor sponsoring terror in Ukraine. The next hearing is due to be held at the International Criminal Court in The Hague.

The effort to document abuses against Ukrainians was initiated by a member of the European Parliament; Polish police have since interviewed and recorded testimony from more than 60 people who were tortured.

After her release Iryna went first to Mariupol and then to Kyiv. Coming to terms with what had happened was agonising; she had to ask herself how to live on. In her native Yasynuvata she had a house with a garden she tended, trees and flowers she had planted, pets and an aquarium. She always believed the Ukrainian army would liberate her town. When the power failed she would climb out of the basement between bombardments to pump oxygen into the fish tank with a bicycle pump so the fish might survive until the army arrived. She had been the first woman in Yasynuvata to learn to drive.

Iryna was active in local life. She organised eight trips to Bavaria for children from Chernobyl-affected families who had settled in the area. When the Russians began occupying Donetsk region she helped Ukrainian servicemen: she cooked with other women to feed soldiers, and during deliveries of humanitarian aid she photographed the supplies so donors could see where their money went. Those images—stored on her tablet—later became evidence of the scale of need and the work volunteers were doing.

Iryna and her fellow volunteers often invited Ukrainian soldiers to Yasynuvata, telling them they must visit her house because she would welcome them under the Ukrainian flag. Seeing how poorly clothed the men were, she raised money to buy uniforms; if they needed blankets or pillows she delivered those too. She and her friends brought food, medicine, cigarettes and household supplies to the Armed Forces. For that work she was arrested.

They came for her while she was in her garden on 14 August 2014. Eight armed men immediately began interrogating her, demanding the names and addresses of local volunteers who were helping the army. They ransacked her home and found records of the funds she had raised for uniforms. She was then taken to Donetsk and held in former military barracks, in cells with bars, where she was beaten and tortured. Again they demanded names and addresses; Iryna gave only the details of people she knew had already left Yasynuvata, and no one was harmed as a result.

While interrogating and beating Iryna they repeated the same threat: 'If you cooperate with us, we will simply shoot you and bury you. If not—you saw a hundred Chechens and Cossacks on the first floor… you might survive a couple of nights…' She was terrified. They ransacked the safe in her home and seized documents proving ownership of her beauty salon, her mother's flat in Yasynuvata and her house—and they knew about her bank account. They demanded she transfer everything into the name of a person they nominated. When she protested that the money belonged to her husband, their reply was chillingly cynical: 'In that case we will send him a video with you in it and he will bring us the money in his teeth.' Iryna knew they meant it.

Later she said that being tied to the pole was, perversely, one of the easier tortures she endured. The public humiliation was awful: people spat at her, pushed and struck her. A 70-year-old woman beat her with a crutch for a long time, shouting 'Fascist, murderer!'; another woman pressed two tomatoes into her eyes. Young people laughed and took selfies with her in the background. Not a single passer-by offered even silent sympathy—perhaps because ten Ossetian soldiers with machine-guns stood close by.

At the time of writing (2025), roughly three hundred Ukrainians are held in prisons in the temporarily occupied Donetsk and Luhansk regions, and new names are added to that list every day.

Iryna Dovhan was given the unofficial title 'People's Hero of Ukraine' in March 2016. She still keeps in touch with some neighbours and knows what became of her house: it was looted by the Vostok Battalion, then taken over as a base by Buryat militias. The Buryat commander liked the house so much he moved his family in—his wife, two children and his parents—and they later had another baby. They even used Iryna's granddaughter's buggy to take the infant out; many of the children's things left in the house proved useful to them.

The garden was neglected. Only in summer was there a beaten path through the high grass to the peach tree; the rest of the fruit trees had been felled to make space for cars the occupiers appear to have requisitioned and stored there.

Iryna and her family had begun to rebuild their life in Kyiv when Russia launched its full-scale invasion on 24 February 2022.

Based on Suspilne Donbas, 22 January 2022 https://suspilne.media/donbas/198390-foto-vratuvalo-meni-zitta-istoria-volonterki-irini-dovgan/; Censor.net https://uaheroes.com/story/iryna-dovhan/ ; *and other sources*

Escape from occupied Kherson—an aunt's story

This is what happened on 20 June 2022 in occupied Kherson. Late that night Kateryna's sister-in-law received a message that someone was breaking down Kateryna's door, but a curfew prevented her from going straight away. When she reached the house early the following morning she found that Kateryna had been raped and tortured to death; a cable tie was fastened round her neck. Her three-year-old son lay nearby.

It was clearly not a robbery: Kateryna's mobile phone, laptop and bank cards were untouched, and her car stood in the yard with the key in the ignition. They had come to kill. Kateryna lay on the sofa in an unnatural position, her head twisted as if her neck had been broken; she was naked and covered in extensive bruising.

The child was also badly injured—his body bore numerous bruises and cigarette burns on his face, temple and forehead. Although his mother was dead, his body was still warm; a tight noose had been placed round his neck and his skin showed signs of severe swelling and bruising. Her sister-in-law, frantic, tried to revive him, shouting, 'Breathe, breathe, live! I won't live without you!'

And then the boy began to breathe.

They were her brother's family—a happy household who loved one another. They had a comfortable home and plans for the future; Kateryna had wanted another child. Then the full-scale war came. Her husband went to the front, leaving his wife and son behind, and Kherson fell under occupation. Kateryna was murdered in her own home.

The sister-in-law later said the neighbours must have heard the screams—it was summer, the windows were broken and open—yet no one came. She called her brother in shock and, at his request, took photographs of the scene to document that Kateryna had died as the result of torture and rape. The child had witnessed the attack and was himself brutally beaten; the assailants had pressed out cigarette butts on his face and neck. A cable tie had been fastened tightly round Kateryna's throat; she lay naked and extensively bruised, her head twisted as if her neck had been broken.

Medical personnel who later examined the boy found him in profound shock. His pulse had stopped and he required urgent resuscitation—clinicians later described a period of clinical death. Officials who attended the scene, including the chief physician and the garrison commander, reacted callously, making cruel remarks about the child's condition.

It is a terrible, intimate cruelty: a family's life destroyed in their own home, a child left with injuries and memories that may never heal.

The aunt decided to flee Kherson as soon as she could conceal the marks of torture on her nephew's face and neck; she was terrified for their lives. Over two weeks she managed to disguise the injuries with make-up so the Russians would not recognise them.

They drove for three days—an 850-kilometre journey to Odesa that required numerous detours and the passage of some thirty Russian checkpoints. At one point the traffic stretched for eighteen kilometres. It was baking hot; some people died in their cars, and others—a man with epilepsy, a woman who had suffered a stroke—collapsed and did not survive the ordeal.

All the way the aunt carried a terrible secret: she was trying to get out with a child who had nearly died from beating and torture. She had false documents and pretended the boy was her own. At the checkpoint before the so-called 'grey zone' their car was halted and she heard one Russian guard say to another, 'These people should be finished off…' The other replied, 'I've had enough for today.' The first persisted, 'I'm fine, I can continue.' The other finally shrugged, 'Oh, let them go. Let the next checkpoint have the fun.' Nearby she saw bodies—at least four—strewn by the roadside. And he did not see how they had died, only that they were dead.

Against all odds, they managed to escape. By the third day of driving the aunt's right leg had become paralysed and she had to operate the pedals with her left leg. She had diabetes and her blood-sugar level reached a critical point—there was no insulin in occupied Kherson—and her blood pressure soared above 200. Still, she vowed she would get them out; so much depended on her, and she promised herself the child would survive. And he did.

The boy cried constantly on the journey, pleading for his mother and begging to be taken home. Before the atrocity he had been an exceptionally bright three-year-old: he had taught himself the Ukrainian and English alphabets from the internet, knew the planets of the solar system—their colours, sizes and distances from the Sun—and displayed a very high aptitude for learning.

After the assault he stopped speaking: his jaw muscles had been damaged, making some sounds and words difficult. His speech development was delayed for about a year, and he had suffered asphyxia. A child's brain is very vulnerable to oxygen loss, and stress can further suppress breathing and impair speech.

In Odesa the doctors diagnosed clinical death, cerebral swelling, an injured right wrist, jaw trauma and displaced teeth. Dentists fitted eight crowns and rebuilt his four front teeth. Although he did not speak for more than a year initially, with sustained psychological support he has made good progress. Two years on, he can ask and answer questions; the principal task now is to restore his spoken language. His aunt believes he will be able to start school at six like any other child.

Source: Suspilne Odesa, 19 March 2024. www.youtube.com/watch?v=DAz7zaGklEo

Notes:
Names have been changed for understandable reasons. Kherson was occupied by Russia from March until 11 November 2022, when it was liberated by the Ukrainian forces.

Oleshky

Oleshky, a town in Kherson region on the eastern bank of the Dnipro opposite Kherson city, was occupied on the very first day of the full-scale invasion. Early on 22 February 2022, at around 07:00, columns of Russian military hardware rolled into the town. Their first task seemed to be to erase any sign of Ukraine: they tore down flags and symbols and announced they had come to stay, promising a 'new life' under new authorities. From the outset they tried to win—or force—local support, using severe punishment for anyone who refused to collaborate.

The account that follows is based on the anonymous testimony of a female resident interviewed by Radio Svoboda; she later escaped the occupied territory.

Until the end of May 2022—nearly three months—shops stood empty. As well as acute shortages, the occupiers practised systematic looting: cars were seized, the best houses requisitioned, and Russian troops took whatever they fancied whenever units rotated. Nothing was sacred—kettles, clothes on washing lines, household goods were simply taken. For residents it felt like savagery; something utterly incongruous in the 21st century.

Round-ups became routine and people lived in terror. Those who refused to collaborate could be detained and face draconian sentences—in some cases up to 20 years in a strict-regime camp. Collaborators, meanwhile, were able to denounce neighbours and settle personal scores; an accusation was enough to trigger interrogation, first in Skadovsk, then Crimea, and often deportation to Russian prisons. There was no pretence of proper investigation—it felt eerily like Stalinist times.

As ever, Russian propaganda targeted the young. The occupiers used a mixture of intimidation and incentives: parents were pressured to send their children to Russian schools and offered 40,000 roubles as a reward, or payments for placing children in Russian holiday camps. Many parents who agreed later discovered they could not get their children back—the youngsters had been taken into Russia.

The occupiers also treated the life of the town as a grim game of 'Russian roulette'. Patrols would turn up at random, position Grad launchers and mortars, fire towards Kherson and then swivel to shell Oleshky, blaming the Ukrainian army for the devastation. Locals knew who was responsible. At Easter, for example, soldiers emplaced artillery in the town centre; after firing at Kherson they began targeting civilians in Oleshky, killing and wounding people and setting buildings alight.

One particularly cruel episode involved a man killed in a mortar strike. His wife gathered the remains in a bag to bury him decently, but the occupiers seized the bag, saying they would take it to Kakhovka for 'examination'. They withheld the body for weeks until she paid a large sum (30–40,000 roubles), money the community helped to raise. Even then they demanded she sign a statement blaming the Ukrainian army for her husband's death. Reluctantly, and under duress, she signed—a final indignity forced on a grieving widow.

The occupiers singled out local people with a pro-Ukrainian stance for particular cruelty. Officially such people were said to be sent west, to the right bank of Kherson region, but eyewitnesses maintain that many never reached that destination alive.

The witness herself was taken to one of the notorious interrogation 'basements' and subjected to electric torture after she refused to collaborate. Four people had recommended her as a competent professional and the occupiers dangled a very high salary and substantial perks to tempt her to cooperate. When she declined—careful to be polite, because she knew 'no' would not be accepted—the beatings began. She was struck with the butt of a rifle across the face, back and collarbone; physical assaults alternated with repeated interrogations.

On at least one occasion they put a heavy iron bracelet on her, poured an unidentified liquid and applied electric current until she fainted: she described hearing a crack and a rising whine as the current intensified. On regaining consciousness she was set upon again. The torture left her with a concussion and a stammer; she later required several operations. Despite renewed offers of cooperation, her refusal only brought further torture.

One morning she woke in a stable. She could hear animals and horses, smell blood and hear inhuman screams. Terrified, she was certain she would die. Then she overheard one occupier say to another, 'Take her round the corner and let's go and eat.' A moment later a voice groaned, 'Around the corner—to shoot you.' In an instant she understood she had only minutes to live. Her only thought was: who would look after her parents and her child?

An idea struck her. She knew the occupiers adored the Soviet past. Her grandfather had been a soldier in the Second World War and had medals and a commendation signed by Marshal Konev. Weak and barely able to speak, she summoned the last of her strength and said, 'Aren't you ashamed? My grandfather fought in the war. Konev himself presented him with a certificate in Red Square.' The eldest of the occupiers seemed impressed. She gave him her grandfather's name; he went away to check. When he returned he ordered her released.

She could not tell how much time had passed—every minute there felt endless—but the command came: 'No corner. Take her and drop her off at the police station.' They bundled her into a car and dumped her at the station without even removing the bag from her head or the tape from her hands.

Her troubles did not end there. Neighbours had reported her for refusing to send her daughter to a Russian school. She had hidden the child at their dacha outside town to keep her safe, but after the concussion and her disappearance the family feared she was dead. The child developed heart problems from the stress and needed care; the occupiers discovered that the girl had not been attending the Russian school and took her to a 'basement' for interrogation.

At first no one could leave Oleshky—evacuation only became possible after the destruction of the Kakhovka hydroelectric station and the subsequent flooding. There was no legal route out: Russian passports were required but the family did not have them. They had never applied for humanitarian aid from the occupiers, because doing so immediately put your details into the passport-registration system. Since the start of the occupation, forced 'passportisation' has been systematically imposed across occupied Ukrainian territory.

In the early hours of 6 June 2023—at around 03:00—the dam of the Kakhovka hydroelectric station in Kherson region was blown up. The plant had been under Russian control since 24 February the previous year. The resulting surge raised water levels and flooded settlements along the Dnipro. Multiple experts have concluded that the breach was most likely caused by explosives planted at the station. The Russian occupation authorities blamed Ukrainian strikes—alleging Vilkha missiles had damaged the dam—but even the Russian state news agency TASS later reported that the cause of the breach could not be attributed to shelling by either side.

The Russian military have made it common practice to direct drones and missiles at civilians and civilian infrastructure—hospitals, schools, nurseries, and energy and water-supply facilities—even as the leadership denies responsibility. After the flood the family tried several times to leave Oleshky; on the last attempt they set out with their neighbours. At a checkpoint the soldiers separated the elderly and children into one group and the adults into another; the adults were taken away for filtration. The family, however, managed to stay together and escape. Others say they were taken to Zalizny Port (Iron Port) or to Skadovsk and held for months—apparently used as human shields in case of a Ukrainian counter-offensive following the Kakhovka dam breach.

Locals recall that, before the dam was destroyed, occupiers shot at privately owned boats and requisitioned the best craft for themselves. When the flood came, Oleshky was underwater within minutes; waters rose to the fourth floor of some buildings and many people drowned. Some residents had hidden boats and used them to rescue neighbours; others lashed planks into makeshift rafts and pulled people to safety. To grasp the scale of the catastrophe, imagine being stranded in the middle of a vast body of water with no shore in sight. Over the following two days roughly 600–700 bodies were recovered and buried.

Survivors say the occupiers dug a large pit on wasteland in Oleshky and dumped corpses there—both people and animals—and another mass grave was reportedly created near Radynske. Bulldozers and tractors were used to move the bodies; locals are certain there are at least two mass graves.

The witness managed to evacuate to the territory under the Ukrainian control together with her family but up to this day she is still afraid and has nightmares about her life in Russian occupied territory.

At the moment (2025) Oleshky is 90% destroyed by bombs and there is no water, no electricity and no gas there. The witness's two houses have been destroyed. And there is no way she would go back there while the war goes on.

Source: Radio Svoboda 7 May 2025. News of the Azov region by Daryna Dovgopyata, https://www.radiosvoboda.org/a/novyny-pryazovya-oleshky-istoriya-zhyttya-v-okupatsiyi/33405965.html

Escape through the Minefield

She managed to evacuate to Ukrainian-held territory with her family, but even now she is haunted by nightmares about life under occupation....

As of 2025 Oleshky lies about 90% destroyed by bombardment; there is no running water, electricity or gas. Both of the witness's houses were destroyed, and she has no intention of returning while the war continues.

Before the war, 36-year-old Tetyana Marvinetska and her family lived in Kherson city; her parents had a house about 20 km away. Their life was ordinary and content—two homes, good jobs, a happy family. Tetyana worked as an anaesthetist in a private clinic. Then Russia launched its full-scale invasion and everything changed.

The Russians occupied Kherson quickly. Tetyana moved immediately to her parents' house, believing it would be safer because it had a cellar for sheltering from shelling. A week later the village was occupied too. The situation deteriorated: they had to travel to Kherson for groceries and, above all, bread, but at times the occupiers simply would not let them through the checkpoints. People were dragged from their cars, subjected to humiliating searches and then turned away without explanation. Tetyana knew how precarious it was—if the soldiers took a dislike to you, they would not hesitate to shoot. Approaching each checkpoint made her heart pound; there were three checkpoints on the 20 km road between the village and Kherson, and the worst was between Chernobayivka and Kherson, which many drivers tried to avoid by crossing the fields.

Before long, their village was on the front line. The occupiers deployed Grad and Uragan rocket systems just two kilometres away, and military convoys rumbled through the streets as Russian forces pushed west towards Mykolaiv.

Shells screamed over their house; everything around them shook. Shooting, explosions and fires raged on both sides. There was no electricity, no water, no work and no food. The final straw was word that the Russians planned to take children away—reportedly to Crimea, supposedly for schooling. That terrified Tetyana, and the family decided they had to leave for somewhere safer. They knew the route might be shelled, but staying amid the fighting under occupation felt far worse.

So Tetyana set off with her two children—Timur, nine, and Viktoriya, seventeen—together with her parents. The godmother of her children, also called Tetyana, joined them with her own two children, aged five and nine. Tetyana's husband did not go: he chose to stay behind, waiting for the moment the Ukrainian Armed Forces might advance so he could rejoin them.

They were not alone. In total seventeen cars left the village that morning, filled with children, the elderly and others desperate to flee. There was no official 'green corridor'—indeed, none existed across Kherson region—but several columns of civilian vehicles had already risked the fields the previous day and made it through. When Tetyana phoned those who had gone ahead and heard they were safe, she found the courage to go.

The whole journey was supposed to be short—about an hour to reach Ukrainian-held territory. The convoy passed two villages without incident, then halted at a Russian checkpoint. The occupiers kept them there for hours, blocking the road with something like a large shell and saying they could go no further. Children climbed out and played; there was a child in every car and two or three in some. One vehicle carried three children and a baby, whose mother was feeding him in full view of the soldiers.

Eventually the Russians allowed them to continue, directing the lead driver along a farm track and naming the settlements ahead. The soldiers assured him that locals used that route daily to deliver milk to Mykolaiv. Six cars turned back, but Tetyana, the Kovtun family and the others pressed on. Their destination felt tantalisingly close.

What they did not know was that the route led straight into a minefield. When the cars did not immediately explode, the soldiers opened fire with grenade launchers. One shell struck Tetyana's car near the left wheel, lifting it into the air and flipping it over, hurling its occupants in different directions.

Tetyana could not remember exactly how the firing began, but Tetyana Kovtun saw the first explosion from her car. She heard a terrible roar to the left and looked round to find a cloud of dust and lumps of earth flying through the air. Then a second blast came from the right. She hugged her children tight and told them to lie on the floor of the car.

Peering through the smoke, she could just make out Tetyana's car, its headlights dim through the haze. The doors were open, but there was no sign of anyone— something terrible had happened.

When Tetyana came to, the only thing she could focus on was her children. Her son lay on the ground, unconscious; her mother sat motionless at the wheel. Tetyana crawled across the wreckage and dragged her son free. She tried to lift him but realised she could not manage alone. 'Viko, help me!' she called to her daughter. The nearest village was only 250 metres away; there was no visible sign of mines in their path, so Tetyana ran, shouting for help.

Together with her daughter, she carried Timur to the village. She laid him on the asphalt and screamed for assistance. Ukrainian soldiers came running, scooped Timur up and rushed him to hospital—exposing themselves to enemy fire in the process of saving others.

Tetyana and her children spent a long time in hospital. Timur had no memory of the attack; he was unconscious for a long while. Viktoriya remembered everything but would not speak about it.

When the Ukrainian forces pushed the occupiers back and Kherson and the village were liberated, Tetyana learned that both her parents had died. She believes her mother remained alive in the car for some time, but no one could reach her because of the incessant shelling.

Some naive observers might claim the Russians did not know there were children in the cars. That is impossible: the soldiers had seen the children during the long delay at the checkpoint, and the travellers had draped white sheets around their vehicles with the word 'Children' written on them. What kind of 'liberators' are these? From what were the Russians 'liberating' Ukrainians—their homes, their futures, their children?

Source: Interview by Olena Bondarenko in TEXTY.ORG.
UA 20 June 2022 https://texty.org.ua/articles/107011/
rosijski-soldaty-zahnaly-ljudej-iz-ditmy-na-minne-pole-i-obstriljaly-z-hranatometiv/

Children of the War

Ivan's Story

Ivan was seven when Russia occupied Luhansk in 2014, so he grew up under occupation from early childhood. He remembers sitting next to his parents as they watched TV and seeing their faces go suddenly tense and worried. He didn't understand what was happening at the time, but within days his parents had packed and the family moved to stay with Ivan's grandmother. While they were away their house was struck by a missile; when they returned and saw the damage, the occupation had truly begun.

Ivan's parents told him that war had started and—falsely—that the Ukrainian Armed Forces had fired rockets at their home. They moved back into Ivan's grandfather's flat in the city because the family felt it was too dangerous to remain where they were. Ivan's grandfather, a priest, writer and lecturer at Luhansk Taras Shevchenko University and a well-known figure in the city, refused to live under occupation; he left Luhansk for the Dnipropetrovsk region because his life was at risk. He invited Ivan's parents to join him, but they refused. In fact, Ivan's parents supported Russia. Their house was later dismantled by the occupiers.

Ivan had completed his first year at a Ukrainian school before the Russian occupation. He remembered the Ukrainian flag flying on 1 September at the start of the school year—the last time he saw that flag until he returned to Ukraine eleven years later. From his second year the curriculum changed: Ukrainian history, language and literature were phased out. At first there was one lesson a week, but after Year 7 those subjects disappeared entirely. Tuition was delivered in Russian, using textbooks brought in from Russia.

Teachers who refused to collaborate left; those who stayed were overworked, nervous and often lost their temper with pupils. The quality of teaching fell, replaced by propaganda: children were told Ukraine was to blame for the fighting and that Kyiv was shelling them—an explanation that made no sense to those who could see the destruction around them. The authorities never called the region Ukrainian territory; it was always the 'LPR'.

Ivan's parents professed to be Ukrainians but supported the LPR. They would say: 'We are good Ukrainians, unlike those in Lviv who support Kyiv. It would be ideal if everyone in Ukraine were like us.' Moving the family to Russia was not an option—they could not afford it, and they feared being treated as outsiders there, laughed at or humiliated, with poor job prospects.

Once the family was travelling to Rostov, across the border into southern Russia, Ivan took three books with him. One was in Ukrainian—Shadows of Forgotten Ancestors by Mykhailo Kotsiubynskyi. He hadn't thought about the consequences of carrying it. At the Russian checkpoint a border guard spotted the books in the car and began to flick through them. He skimmed the Russian titles and then reached the Ukrainian one. A second guard joined him, then a senior officer. The mood changed.

'What is this?' the officer asked.

'Just a book to read,' Ivan replied.

'Don't you know it's forbidden to bring those books into Russia?'

'It's only to pass the time.'

'Do you understand you're going to have problems? We're going to take you to speak to an FSB man.'

Ivan, though only fifteen at the time, understood the gravity of the situation—and his parents did too. The guards took his parents into a room to talk while he waited in the car. When they returned they were agitated: they had been allowed to pass only on condition that the book be disposed of. At a nearby bin they tore out pages and hurled the remainder away. Only then were they permitted to continue. The officers had been incredulous that a teenager from the LPR would be carrying a Ukrainian book—let alone intending to read it.

What they did not know was that Ivan's grandfather had been a highly educated man with a large private library. Hidden among his things were books about the 1932–33 Ukrainian famine, the Ukrainian Insurgent Army and Stepan Bandera. Ivan, curious, had read them.

In 2019 Ivan began to make friends online with youngsters in Dnipro. It started by accident: someone in a chat joked about the Luhansk region and Ivan, intrigued, wanted to know more. He assumed they were local and that they might meet up, but then discovered they were from Dnipro. They started talking and remain in contact to this day—a friendship that began when Ivan was twelve and they were thirteen. Ivan remembers joking, 'You're really from Dnipro? Then we must be enemies.'

They replied: 'Why would we be enemies? You're from Ukraine and so are we.'

'I'm from the LPR—why do you call me Ukrainian?' Ivan shot back.

That kicked off long conversations about the occupation, the Revolution of Dignity in 2014 and the ATO. To prove their points, his Dnipro friends began sending him videos and news links from Ukrainian and Western sources. For the first time Ivan was able to compare the Russian messaging he'd grown up with against alternative accounts. The contrast was stark. Where he had once accepted the pro-Russian line, doubts began to take root.

Those online friendships also helped him learn Ukrainian. Before the full-scale invasion his friends had spoken Russian in daily life; when the war started they switched to Ukrainian—and Ivan followed their example. Gradually he began to speak and read Ukrainian more confidently.

At school the indoctrination continued. His history teacher claimed that, during the Second World War, Hitler's troops had not attacked Lviv—an assertion presented to suggest that Ukrainians had somehow supported the Third Reich. The effect was to foster a narrative that Ukrainians were all 'Nazis', a caricature that made little sense to Ivan once he could see other sources and hear different stories from his friends.

In their minds, Lviv and western Ukraine were 'Bandera territory'. Ivan never heard about much of Ukraine's wider history—not the Zaporizhian Host (the Cossack army of the 15th–18th centuries defeated under Catherine II), not the Hetmanate (the Ukrainian polity of 1649–1764 that was gradually absorbed by the Russian Empire), nor the Principality of Galicia–Volhynia (1199–1349). According to the official line they were taught, those chapters of Ukrainian history either never happened or were simply part of Russian history. It was as if Ukraine, as a distinct nation, did not exist at all.

They were, however, taught about Kyivan Rus: Prince Volodymyr's adoption of Christianity in 988 and Yaroslav the Wise (c. 983–1054), whose daughters married kings in France, Norway and Hungary. Even here, though, the curriculum insisted these were essentially Russian princes—despite the fact that Moscow was not founded until 1147. Even local Turkic artefacts, such as the Polovtsian stone idols in the Luhansk region, were presented as part of a supposed great Russian culture.

Unsurprisingly, the pupils learned the anthem of the Luhansk People's Republic; in the senior classes they were also taught the Russian anthem.

They were eventually compelled to stop singing the LPR anthem and, over time, to sing only the Russian anthem.

In 2021 Ivan and his family moved to the Moscow region. He had been studying at a secondary school in Luhansk, but an LPR school certificate would get him nowhere: it was not recognised in Ukraine and carried little weight elsewhere, so he could practically only go on to a university inside the LPR. His parents wanted to give him better prospects—both an education recognised in Russia and a chance of work there—so, when Ivan was in the 9th form they pulled him out of school in Luhansk and took him to finish his education in Russia with a school-leaving certificate that would be accepted more widely.

The first Russian school they approached refused to admit him. Four more turned them away for the same reason: 'Why did you come here? Your education there is at a very low level.' When staff looked at his school report they scoffed at his modest marks: 'What are you doing here? Look at your grades.' In the end one school did accept him—fortunately an excellent one. Ivan remembers his first day: during a break the teacher brought him into the classroom and said, 'This is Ivan. He's new and will study with you.' The response was muted; the others were talking, so Ivan sat down and waited. After a while some boys came over and asked, 'Where are you from?'

Ivan didn't want to admit he was from the LPR, so he said simply that he came from Luhansk. 'Where's that?' the boys asked. 'In Ukraine,' he shrugged. 'Ah, OK,' they said.

He felt like an outsider in the class: they had all known one another since the first year and were slow to include the newcomer. The curriculum was tougher too, and he found the work hard.

On the morning the full-scale invasion began in February 2022, Ivan was getting ready for school when he saw Putin on every channel. He messaged his friends: 'How are you?' and got the reply, 'Lots of explosions—war has broken out.' When he told his classmates at school, many barely reacted. 'Oh, don't worry—it'll stop soon. Everything will be fine,' they laughed; they treated him as if he were overreacting. Later, after seeing the horrors at Mariupol and Bucha, Ivan felt only anger. His classmates' indifference—'Yes, there's a war. So what?'—filled him with bitterness.

At the start of the invasion, many Ukrainian websites were blocked, but news was still available on YouTube and Telegram. Ivan followed channels such as Sternenko's. He also learned about the so-called 'basements'—secret cells and torture chambers used in Luhansk for political prisoners and those who opposed the occupation. One notorious site was the former SBU building, now reportedly used by the FSB, whose cellars were said to be used for interrogations and torture; if someone was taken there, it often took a miracle to survive.

When the family returned from the Moscow region, Ivan's parents were once taken in for interrogation. The trouble began over a parking space outside their five-storey block: their new neighbour, it turned out, was a Russian serviceman who had taken the spot. Ivan's father went to argue the point. Not long after, four men knocked at the family's door and led both parents to the notorious building. Their phones were seized and examined and they were questioned for two hours.

The interrogators found no overtly pro-Ukrainian material, but still tried to trap them with questions. 'Why isn't your son fighting in the army?' they demanded. 'He's only fifteen,' his parents replied. Only then were they released. They left shaken—during the interrogation they had heard the cries of other people being tortured in the building. Had the officers found messages between Ivan and his friends in Dnipro on his phone, the consequences might well have been fatal.

Strangely, despite the ordeal, Ivan's parents later became friendly with the Russian neighbour.

In 2022 Ivan returned to Luhansk and enrolled at the Luhansk Academy. After the full-scale invasion his plans to leave hardened: he knew he had to move quickly to avoid being mobilised into the LPR forces. He took work, saved diligently and researched the documents he would need. The only practical way to get a Ukrainian biometric passport was via the Ukrainian embassy in Minsk, so he told his parents he needed a Russian passport to travel abroad. His mother was resigned; his father insisted he could only go as far as Rostov.

Ivan contacted the Children's Rights Ombudsman, who confirmed he could travel to Belarus as soon as he turned eighteen. On the morning of his birthday, 12 January, he slipped away to Rostov. He bought a return ticket to Luhansk for 15 January, a bus ticket to Moscow that evening and onward train travel to Minsk. He even took a selfie in Rostov to prove he'd been there.

At 05:00 on 13 January he was at the train station in Minsk waiting for the embassy to open. For the first time since the seventh form he heard Ukrainian spoken again. The embassy staff questioned him in Ukrainian; nervous, he replied in Russian and explained that he was there to obtain a biometric passport. When they asked for his Ukrainian passport he produced only his Russian passport and birth certificate. 'You are a Russian citizen—what are you doing here?' they asked. He said the Ombudsman had authorised the trip.

After a tense wait of about two hours, the embassy issued his first Ukrainian passport. From Minsk he travelled on to Dnipro, where his friends were waiting to meet him.

Shortly after he arrived his mother phoned, desperate to know where he was. When Ivan told her he was in Ukraine, his father reacted angrily—hurling insults and denouncing Ukraine. His mother was distraught; she accused him of abandoning and betraying her, burst into tears and could not understand his decision. Ivan, by contrast, was elated to be in Ukraine. His grandfather, whom he had not seen since 2014, was stunned when Ivan rang; it took almost a week for him to accept that it really was his grandson. When they finally met they talked for hours, trying to make up for the eleven years apart. Not long afterwards his grandfather had to flee again as Russian forces drew nearer to where he was staying in Dnipropetrovsk region; he is now near Vinnytsia while Ivan is in Kyiv. Ivan had imagined life in Kyiv would be calm, but there are regular missile and drone attacks—something he had not experienced in Luhansk since active fighting ceased there in 2014.

Kateryna's story

Kateryna was seven when Donetsk fell under Russian control in 2014. She still remembers the panic of her parents when the war began—she could not then comprehend what it meant, but the fear remains vivid. Her parents hurriedly told her and her brother to pack the most important things. The house became a scene of chaos. Kateryna, her mother and her grandmother fled to Russia and lived in Rostov until things quietened in Donetsk and the surrounding area.

In Rostov she attended a Russian school while her mother worked. She stayed there until the fourth form. At first the other children treated her as different; later they accepted her, but she found it hard to switch to Russian. She could not understand why she had to learn it and was sometimes teased for a Ukrainian accent— especially for her pronunciation of the 'g' sound. She missed her home in Donetsk.

When the situation seemed to have stabilised they returned to Donetsk and Kateryna resumed school there. Up to the seventh grade she had some Ukrainian lessons, but after that all subjects were taught in Russian. Having known no other life as a child, she accepted that as normal. It was like being a caged animal that has been kept in captivity all its life and comes to see that life as natural. The occupiers exploited the language issue: they warned people that if you did not speak Russian you would not be respected in Ukraine, and they told stories of Russian-speaking people from Kharkiv who allegedly fared badly in the west. What they did not mention was how they were devastating Russian-speaking cities such as Mariupol, or the daily bombardment of Kharkiv. Instead, the message was constant: the Ukrainian army was shelling Donbas and killing civilians—and many people believed it.

From the tenth grade there was a compulsory subject called Basic Military Training, where pupils were taught to march and to handle weapons. The teacher wore camouflage and acted like a military commander issuing orders to children—a practice reminiscent of Soviet schools before the USSR collapsed.

There was also a lesson titled 'Talk about Important Things'. Each class would begin by standing to sing the Russian anthem, then learn patriotic songs and listen to praise of the Russian army and the motherland. Over time Kateryna stopped attending these lessons; she feared the propaganda might influence her. Many pupils regularly skipped lessons and the teachers often looked the other way, since it was not the only subject that was dodged. Strangely, though, some girls were keen to join the army and go to the front, while others resolved to study medicine so they could help soldiers in future. For boys there seemed to be only two real-istic options: university or war—because in Donetsk, in practice, only servicemen earned a decent living; in most other jobs it was impossible to make enough money to live without worry.

As a teenager Kateryna made many friends in online chats and became curious about life beyond the occupied territory. Her contacts included young people from Ukraine, Belarus and Russia—and, to her surprise, many teenagers in Russia expressed support for Ukraine. Her parents warned her to be extremely cautious online: they begged her never to post in Ukrainian because, they said, a single message might trigger a report that would put not only her but the whole family at risk.

Kateryna made a friend in Kyiv who was a little older than her, and their conver-sations fascinated her. He had been older when the war began and could explain things she barely understood. He described events in Kyiv and how the conflict had unfolded in Donetsk in a way that made sense to her, and the puzzle pieces began to fall into place. She learned about Bucha, Mariupol and other towns levelled by the Russians.

Kateryna tried to raise these discoveries with her parents but quickly saw they either didn't know or simply didn't want to talk about it; they were anxious and preferred to keep silent. They warned her not to mention such things anywhere—they were afraid of the consequences and understood the danger. When Russia organised a referendum to suggest local support for the occupation, turnout was low. Kateryna's parents did not vote—though they publicly professed pro-Russian sympathies—and Kateryna could not vote because she was underage. Rumour had it that those who opposed the vote later suffered: soldiers would come to their homes and threaten them with weapons.

With help from a children's rights organisation and its volunteers, Kateryna managed to leave Donetsk and settle in Kyiv. They found her a hostel, took in a child with no money and guaranteed her anonymity while she got her bearings. She met the friend from her online chat again—they argued about politics at first, but calmed down and reconciled.

Kateryna now feels free in Kyiv despite the missile strikes. She can speak Ukrainian here, which would have been impossible in Donetsk, and she no longer feels any inferiority for being from the east or for speaking Russian. She understands now how the Russians used the language issue as a Trojan horse. Life in Kyiv is very different from the sanctioned, Russia-and-Belarus-dependent markets she knew before: there is a greater variety of goods, and Kyiv's universities offer many more courses and the chance to go abroad to study or work.

Sevilia's story

Sevilia was nine when Russia occupied Crimea in 2014. She was at school when an announcement came that there was shooting in the city centre and that parents should collect their children. Lessons were suspended for several days and the pupils were sent home; those days were declared holidays. It was then that the children heard about the arrival of Russian forces and the new authorities taking control.

What actually happened was that Russian troops entered the parliament building in Simferopol and seized power. Everyone followed the events on the news. Sevilia remembers her grandmother sitting in front of the television, crying—not only at the sight of the Russian flags but because those flags recalled the Soviet era and the 1944 deportation of the Crimean Tatars. For her grandmother, it was painfully familiar: the same authorities returning to a place that had already suffered great injustice.

Sevilia was in Year 4 when the occupation began. Children normally had to sit exams before entering Year 5, but those tests were cancelled because the new administration needed to overhaul the school curriculum. When she returned in Year 5 the changes were stark. Ukrainian was removed from the timetable and relegated to an after-school elective once or twice a week. A course in Russian history was introduced and heavy Russian propaganda began to permeate lessons. Ukrainian flags were taken down and replaced by Russian ones, and teaching was switched entirely to Russian. Pupils were told that Russia had reclaimed its historic territory—slogans such as 'Finally, Crimea has come home!' were everywhere. Some children accepted this because their parents echoed the same message; others, including many Ukrainians and Crimean Tatars, saw it for what it was: a plain invasion.

Despite Russian claims that Crimea had been taken 'without a single shot' and welcomed by the population, demonstrations in support of Ukraine did take place. They were soon crushed. People began to disappear, and it became clear that speaking out was no longer safe.

It was the same story as in Kherson after the 2022 occupation: people marched with Ukrainian flags and slogans, then the occupiers answered with gas, gunfire and the disappearance of demonstrators into the notorious 'basement' for interrogation and torture. Likewise, many Crimean Tatars took to the streets to show their opposition—they knew only too well what the new authorities would do. Civil liberties had no place in the Russkiy Mir, the so-called 'Russian World'.

One of the first acts was to silence Tatar media: the only Crimean Tatar television channel had its licence quietly allowed to lapse, and news in the Tatar language was effectively outlawed. Protests in defence of the channel were met with mass detentions. On 18 May, the Day of Deportation—the annual memorial for the 1944 deportation of Crimean Tatars—Russia banned the commemorations that had previously been permitted and supported by Ukraine. Officials gave vague excuses such as 'to prevent rioting' or 'to avoid conflict,' but to Tatars the ban was plainly political: the memorial was an expression of dissent. The authorities kept a tight watch on Tatar districts; people lived under constant surveillance and the sense of control made any public act of remembrance or protest perilous.

Sevilia last sang a Ukrainian song in the fifth grade. Even the idea of anyone singing in Ukrainian would prompt questions—why do that, why promote it? She still remembers the fear in her teachers' eyes. Her music teacher looked terrified when Sevilia sang in Ukrainian; no one said anything, but Sevilia felt the pressure deep in her subconscious. Thoughts ran through her head about what she ought to do and what she ought not to do. Anyone who wanted to sing in Ukrainian risked being questioned: why choose that? She understood then that continuing to sing Ukrainian would invite trouble. Singing in Tatar, by contrast, was tolerated—so long as it caused no resistance; the occupiers only permitted cultural expression that didn't challenge their control.

Sevilia's family, like many Tatar families, refused to leave—Crimea is their homeland. To abandon it would feel like conceding everything they had longed for. The prospect of fleeing a second time was simply not an option: they could not imagine letting the Russians destroy what they had waited so long to reclaim.

They marked every Russian holiday at school—Constitution Day, Remembrance Day and the rest—so, in effect, they lived as if they were already in Russia. At assemblies to celebrate Soviet-era anniversaries, war veterans would be brought in and greeted with great ceremony, just as the pupils had been taught. Sometimes honoured guests arrived from Russia or from Simferopol, where the authorities were fully Russian, or popular Russian singers came to perform in Crimea. Overall the media diet—especially the programmes teenagers watched—was pure Russian propaganda: serials and films from Russia, Russian TikTokers, and so on.

After the annexation many Western brands disappeared—no McDonald's or familiar high-street names—so everything became Russian. Only when Sevilia finally left Crimea did she realise she actually knew more about Russian TV series, films and influencers than Ukrainian ones. In the senior years a cadet class was introduced with the explicit aim of cementing nostalgia for the Soviet Union and the values Russia glorifies. While other classes had PE on the sports field, the cadets practised marching, sang Russian songs and obeyed commands from a military instructor.

If you imagine being subjected to this from childhood, you can see how hard it is for a child to conceive of any alternative view. This generation was raised on relentless Russian propaganda: the national anthem, Second World War songs and stories that present Russia as the sole victor, downplaying allied help. It's hard to imagine how to reach these children after such sustained indoctrination. They were warned off participating in any demonstrations and forced to sign pledges not to protest, on pain of court action; even protests about internal Russian matters were banned and threatened with blacklisting. The message was clear: you are always being watched. At the same time, Russians flowed into Crimea as holidaymakers and settlers; once the Kerch Bridge opened, the peninsula became an easy destination and, in summer, long queues formed at the crossing. Many Russians relocated there, and locals saw packed beaches and holiday parties—often with cheers of 'Finally, we're home!'—which only reinforced the impression that Crimea had been reclaimed.

They also built roads for military vehicles, tanks and other heavy kit, quietly preparing for a large-scale invasion of Ukraine. Much of this equipment arrived at night so people wouldn't notice or panic, and military bases were established across Crimea. At the time, Russia claimed the new roads and the bridge were for holidaymakers and to make travel to the resorts easier—a convenient cover for a far more sinister plan.

Classrooms filled with new pupils whose parents had moved in from elsewhere in Russia, while many Ukrainians left and their homes were handed over to the incomers. Some locals welcomed the change, but others did not. After the full-scale invasion began on 24 February 2022, Sevilia stopped speaking to friends who openly backed Russia; she feels for them now, because only someone repeatedly exposed to that propaganda could come to believe it.

Sevilia's family history makes all this especially painful. Her grandmother, a Crimean Tatar, was deported in 1944—first to Siberia and then to Uzbekistan—and in those early years of exile an estimated 18–46% of Crimean Tatars died. Sevilia herself was not born in Crimea; her family only returned after the Soviet collapse in 1991, when many Tatars came back from across the world. That return was a moment of joy—until Russia came back and began enforcing the same repressive policies that once cost so many lives.

The occupiers have sought to erase Tatar identity: limiting the language, cancelling symbols and cultural institutions, and undermining the community's very existence. As a result, many young Crimean Tatars, including Sevilia, cannot speak their language well—something she deeply regrets. The deportations and the redistribution of houses to Russian soldiers have changed the island's demographic makeup so that a large share of the population now originates from Russia or other parts of the former Soviet Union. To add insult to injury, Russian propaganda has branded Crimean Tatars as traitors—a stigma that many Russians have accepted.

There were severe water shortages in Crimea. Supply ran to a strict timetable, but in high-rise blocks the water often only reached the ground floor. Everyone else had to carry buckets or plastic canisters down to collect what they could and haul it back up—a brutal chore for the elderly, and a heavy burden for young Sevilia when her parents were at work.

Sevilia had always wanted to study in Kyiv. Before the full-scale invasion she visited her brother, who was then a student there, and she made plans to leave Crimea. On 24 February 2022 she was on her way to Bucha to collect a friend so they could go together. As they were leaving the town they saw tanks rolling in— Ukrainian tanks at that stage, since the Russians had not yet occupied Bucha. The sight of so many people desperately trying to flee with their children was terrifying.

After that Sevilia went to Europe. She realised she could not return to Crimea to live again beneath Russian flags or under Russian rule, not after what she had seen and learned about the occupation. She had never imagined such a war could happen in the twenty-first century—it felt absurd in an age of diplomacy and democracy.

And yet the war began and she had to flee Kyiv—but she would never go back to Crimea, the place where it all started in 2014. She knew she could not keep silent there; she could not live under a regime that crushed free speech. It is a tragedy, because Crimea is a singular place with its own history and a healing climate, but the Russians have spoiled it. There is no freedom there, and life without freedom is no life at all—the freedom Ukraine gave her is precious.

For seventeen years Sevilia had not left Crimea. Now she works and travels across Europe. She feels free and is no longer afraid to speak. Freedom of expression, something impossible in Russia, is a simple joy she savours every day. It is wonderful to live openly and to shape your life as you wish—something that was denied to her in Crimea.

Source: interviews by Ramina Eshakzai, Youtube @Raminaeshakzai 20 June 2025, https://youtu.be/PVB18cRlw5w?si=xToS4CkC4OEcaMSK

Section Introduction: Civilians and Soldiers

Previous sections have chronicled civilians fleeing to save their children from war, torture and other violations of human rights in prisons for both POWs and Ukrainian civilians, and the dire and worsening situation in the Russian occupied territories. This short section tells the stories of people from wider society—a young journalist tortured and cruelly killed in a prison camp where she should not have been in the first place, a child's heroism when Russian shells hit the bus he was travelling on with his mother, survivors of the bombing of the Mariupol Drama Theatre, World War Two veterans living through it all again, and a soldier badly injured and left for dead who returned to fight on the front line.[1]

Our major omission is the terrible story of the abducted children. Russia's huge programme of the illegal removal and Russification of large numbers of Ukrainian children is a tragedy. They are dispersed across Russia and rarely returned. There is some official information on www.ukrainianwarstories.com/more-information.

---

1   For newer stories, keep an eye on www.ukrainianwarstories.com, and for the sequel.

Viktoriya Roshchyna. Death in Russian Captivity—A high price for the truth about the Russian war against Ukraine

Viktoriya Roschyna was an experienced freelance journalist who wrote investigations and news pieces for a number of Ukrainian outlets, including Ukrainska Pravda, Hromadske, Ukrainske Radio, UA:Pershyi, Tsenzor.net and Radio Liberty/Radio Free Europe.

Taken captive in late 2023, Viktoriya was placed on a list for return because she was a civilian—and her detention was therefore illegal under the Geneva Conventions. This was not her first brush with Russian captivity: in March 2022 she spent ten days detained in occupied Berdyansk, Zaporizhzhia region. At that time the former Hromadske editor Evgeniya Motorevska (later head of investigations at The Kyiv Independent) played a key role in securing her release.

Viktoriya's work in frontline and occupied areas had been driven by a conviction that keeping lines of communication open with people under occupation was her life's mission. Those first ten days in detention were extremely painful: she endured repeated interrogations and was coerced into recording a video. Brave though she was, she was forced to make the recording—which ultimately amounted to a neutral statement saying she had no complaints against the Russians.

Despite that first brutal detention, Viktoriya kept returning to occupied areas—convinced she could not report properly without seeing things with her own eyes. She listened to people, told their stories and, when safety demanded it, published pieces anonymously. Her reporting was an act of defiance: a gauntlet thrown down at those who seize territory, abduct civilians, torture and brutalise the innocent.

Viktoriya was a careful professional, not a thrill-seeker. She understood the danger; she later told cellmates she knew the FSB had been watching her. She even remembered seeing a drone hover overhead the day a van stopped and she was seized. In July 2023—about a month before her fatal detention—she gave an interview to Voice of America in which she outlined her investigation into the so-called private armies operating under the occupying authorities in Crimea.

On 3 August 2023 Viktoriya vanished while working in the Russian-occupied Zaporizhzhia region. Colleagues later learned she had travelled there to gather material for her investigation; the trip was a secret and only a handful of people knew about it. As a freelancer reporting from occupied areas, she had accepted high personal risk.

In May 2024 the Russian authorities, for the first time, acknowledged they had detained her; the International Committee of the Red Cross also confirmed she had been held in Detention Centre No. 2 in Taganrog, Rostov region—a facility notorious in reports about the mistreatment of Ukrainian detainees. The Russians provided no details about her conditions or the cause of death. We now know she died while being transferred to Moscow before her planned return; she was 27 and had been healthy before captivity.

An official letter from the Russian Ministry of Defence, received by Viktoriya's father, states she died on 19 September 2024 after more than a year in detention. When her remains were returned they were labelled 'unidentified male' and were badly decomposed. The body showed signs consistent with suffocation or strangulation—including a neck fracture—as well as evidence of electric-shock torture to the feet and multiple bruises and cuts. Reports also note that several organs (including the eyes, brain and part of the larynx) were missing, which has been interpreted as an attempt to conceal the cause of death.

Unfortunately, the bodies of Ukrainian prisoners are often returned in such a condition that determining the true cause of death is impossible. Russian autopsy reports commonly cite 'heart failure'—a finding that clumsily tries to mask the physiological collapse caused by prolonged starvation, dehydration or the extreme stress of detention.

Steve Capus, president of Radio Free Europe/Radio Liberty, has called for those responsible for keeping Viktoriya Roschyna in custody to be prosecuted; the Ukrainian Prosecutor General is investigating her death as a war crime. The illegal detention and tragic death of Viktoriya underlines the extreme risks journalists face when they report the truth about Russia's war in Ukraine.

As of 2025, there are reported to be some 186 prisons in Russia and in occupied Ukrainian territory where Ukrainians have been held and mistreated. Around 16,000 Ukrainian civilians are thought to be detained in these facilities—a stark reminder of the human cost of this conflict.

Sources include: https://ua.korrespondent.net/ukraine/events/4722660-vykradena-okupantamy-ukrainska-zhurnalistka-pomerla-v-poloni; https://en.wikipedia.org/wiki/Victoria_Roshchyna.

Kyrylo, a 13 year old Hero

What springs to mind when you hear the word 'hero'? Hercules or Titan, Achilles or Prometheus? A famous boxer, a weightlifter, or even a cartoon caped crusader?

Our real hero comes from Ukraine. His name is Kyrylo Illiashenko. He is just 13 years old, in Year 8 at Sumy High School No. 4, and he trains in freestyle wrestling at a local youth sports school.

Kyrylo became a hero in the most ordinary—and terrifying—way: he saved people from a burning bus. When the passengers were trapped and the door jammed, it was Kyrylo who acted. Brave, calm and quick-thinking, he helped others out of danger when every second counted.

It happened on 13 April 2025 in Sumy, a town in north-east Ukraine—Palm Sunday, an important holy day. People were returning from morning services when, at 10:20, a Russian ballistic missile—packed in a cassette designed to kill as many people as possible—struck the centre of Sumy. Three minutes later, at 10:23, a second missile hit the same area. This cruel tactic—sending a follow-up strike to target those rushing to help the wounded from the first blast—was all too familiar.

There was smoke and fire, crushed glass and dozens of burnt-out cars across the central streets. Bodies lay scattered; blood flowed through the pavements. In total 119 people were wounded (only two were military personnel)—among them 15 children—and 34 people were killed, including two children. A trolleybus running through the centre was burned out; its passengers and the driver were killed inside.

Fifty buildings were destroyed or badly damaged: the Congress Hall of Sumy State University, four educational institutions, apartment blocks, cafés, shops and the City Library, which had hosted children's clubs and workshops. Windows in neighbouring buildings, including the courthouse and several historic structures, were blown out. Because the missiles were equipped with cluster munitions, the devastation and the civilian toll were wide-ranging and indiscriminate.

Kyrylo and his mother Maryna were on a bus visiting his grandmother. They sat together while his mother chatted on the phone about Sunday lunch. Then came a strange whistling sound—and an explosion. Kyrylo was thrown to the bus floor. Smoke filled the vehicle, the windows shattered, and shards of glass rained down on him, cutting his skin. He felt something land on his head; he was covered in broken glass, but there was no time to check. People were shouting for the driver to open the door. Maryna called his name; he shouted back to let her know he was alive. Later they learned the driver had been killed and could not open the door.

When the falling glass finally eased, Kyrylo started to get up and the acrid smell of burning hit him. He understood then that the bus was on fire and they had to get out—if they stayed, they risked burning alive. He tried the rear door but it was jammed by a fallen tree. Adrenaline took over. He grabbed his gym bag—he had planned to go to wrestling practice after lunch—and threw it through a window. Then, without hesitating, he climbed through the same window and landed on the bag.

Kyrylo scrambled out and ran to the front of the bus. From the outside he forced the front door open—no easy task, he later said, and one he believed his wrestling had helped him accomplish—and began hauling people clear. Then he saw his mother: her face was a mask of blood where the glass had sliced her, but she was alive, and that was all that mattered.

Had Kyrylo not acted so quickly and so bravely, everyone on that bus—including his mother—could have burned. His classmates are full of gratitude: he pulled to safety the aunt of one pupil and the grandmother of another, both passengers on that doomed service. Kyrylo himself was wounded, carrying three pieces of shrapnel in his head; surgeons later removed one large fragment, while two others remain lodged deep and will require further operations. Even so, he managed to get himself and others out of the burning vehicle.

Kyrylo did what had to be done. He is a true hero.

Source: based on an article by Daria Shulzhenko in the Kyiv Independent 21.4.2025, https://kyivindependent.com/how-brave-teen-rescued-people-in-sumy-attack/

Mariupol Drama Theatre—the story of a survivor

On 16 March 2022 at 10:00 the Russian military launched an air raid on the Mariupol Drama Theatre. At the time the building served as a civilian shelter and a huge sign painted in white on the square—'Children'—marked its purpose. Estimates vary, but between roughly 300 and 800 people are believed to have died under the rubble. There were almost no combatants in or around the theatre: only people bringing food and water and police trying to keep order. After Russian forces completed the occupation of Mariupol on 20 May 2022, the DPR prosecutor's office claimed an explosive device had detonated inside the building and that 14 bodies had been found during clearance. That account was rejected by international investigators. Amnesty International concluded that the bombs were dropped from an aircraft by the Russian military and called the attack a war crime.

This is the story of Olena Matyushyna, who survived the bombardment. Since 2022 Olena has never forgotten two dates: 24 February, when the full-scale invasion began, and 16 March, her second birthday—the day she lived through the theatre bombing. Survivors keep in touch and mark that date each year; Olena usually spends both anniversaries in church, praying and remembering.

On 24 February 2022 Olena and her husband were woken just before 05:00 by explosions so violent they were thrown to the floor. The shelling was so intense they did not dare leave their home in the eastern district of Mariupol. There was no electricity and no telephone connection. On the third day they moved to Cheremushky, another district of the city, to stay with Olena's 85-year-old mother and their daughter and son-in-law. In Cheremushki Russian missiles struck the building, blowing out windows and doors. People shouted and screamed. Five storeys were gutted and a fierce fire raged all day; they spent hours trying to put it out. When her husband finally returned from work they decided it was too dangerous to remain—later a Russian tank came and drove its barrel through the kitchen window, destroying everything inside.

So Olena, her daughter and son-in-law went to the Drama Theatre in the city centre, where her husband worked as the administrator. They took only documents and a first-aid kit.

When Olena entered the theatre she was horrified. The auditorium, built to seat 600, had had all its chairs removed; people filled every available space—two upper floors, the basement, the stairwells, pressed against walls and lying on the floor. To take a single step you had to step over somebody. Outside it was minus 12°C; there was no heating, no running water and no food. The theatre had become a makeshift refuge for the desperate, and the scale of need—for warmth, for water, for safety—was overwhelming.

Evgeniya Zabolotna, one of the theatre staff, had been chosen by the crowd to take charge. Olena went up to her and asked, 'What shall we do? There are so many people here.' Evgeniya estimated there were about 1,500, and that number was growing by the day. Rumours of a green-corridor evacuation circulated but never came to anything; instead more and more people arrived. It quickly became clear that many needed medical attention—if nothing was done, they would soon be burying people en masse. The refuge was overwhelmingly civilian: mothers with children of all ages, elderly people, and those with disabilities, many without anything resembling proper bedding, just cardboard on the floor. Many had fled bombed houses without warm clothing for the freezing streets. A first-aid post was therefore established in a dressing room on the theatre's first floor.

Her husband went straight to a little storeroom, forced the padlock and hauled the door open. The cupboard was tiny but dry and out of sight of the windows; it smelled faintly of dust and old paint. They dragged a couple of broken chairs inside, laid down a roll of cardboard and wrapped one of the injured children in a blanket. Olena fetched a thermometer and a strip of antiseptic wipes; the nurses—both called Olha—checked the child over while the mother sat with her head in her hands, trembling. The boy, Sashko, had grazes on his knees and a cut behind one ear from glass, and he kept flinching at every distant explosion. Apart from that there were no immediate life-threatening injuries, but Olena knew the invisible wounds—the shock, the hunger, the sleeplessness—could be as dangerous as any shrapnel.

They gave him a small cup of the hot, thin soup from the field kitchen and some paracetamol for the pain. The nurses washed and dressed his cuts with the precious dressing packs; Olena labelled a box for 'Children's wound care' and made a note to check on them through the night. Around them the first aid post hummed with a grim, ad-hoc efficiency: someone stapled up a torn curtain for privacy, another man brought in a bundle of mittens, and the police dripped in with another ration of antibiotics. Outside, the shelling never stopped. Inside, for a few hours at least, a woman and her boy had a corner where someone listened, someone cleaned their wounds and someone promised—quietly, stubbornly—to do what they could.

* * *

Olena would never forget the day the Drama Theatre was bombed. She had woken early to go to her first-aid post but, exhausted, had lain down for a moment and drifted off. It was snowy and bitterly cold outside; her daughter and a friend were boarding up a window with playbills to keep in the heat. When Olena came to she found the girl shaking her and asking, 'Anatoliyivna, are you alive?'

'I am,' Olena replied, and then, still dazed, asked about her daughter. 'She's alive,' came the answer. They were both at the rear of the theatre; the central part had been destroyed—walls and roof had simply collapsed. The air was thick with white dust and smoke and the building rang with terrible, endless screams. Then Olena saw a boy crawling over the rubble, blood streaming down his face and neck. She dropped to her knees to help him. Sashko told her, between sobs, that his mother had been killed. Many of those sheltering near the field kitchen and in the auditorium had not survived.

Everyone in the central part of the theatre had been killed—hundreds of people. Olena's husband and son-in-law had watched the strike and at first believed there could be no survivors. Her husband went hysterical with grief; the police had to disarm him because he was uncontrollable. He was terrified to go near the ruins, crying and screaming in the street. Her son-in-law, though, forced his way through the wreckage and found Olena and his wife alive, and he shouted the news back to the husband. Their neighbour, Olena Kuznetsova, who had been sheltering in a little store cupboard, had been in the field kitchen when the raid hit—she did not survive. No one who had been in the auditorium's centre had made it.

Olena's first thought was for the small boy she had seen before the blast. She climbed through the wreckage to the cupboard where the woman and her twelve-year-old had been sheltering. The boy stood there in a kind of stupor, utterly shocked—not crying, eyes wide and empty, like a statue. His mother lay trapped under the rubble; he could only recognise her by the manicure on her fingers. He had no one else left.

Olena put her arms round him and held him gently. 'Sashenka, you're coming with me,' she told him. 'You'll be with us.'

Then her husband appeared, and it was clear there was nothing left for them in the city. Olena told them they had to go. Outside, the police were beginning the grim work of removing the dead; the wounded were staggering out of the wreckage. It was pure hell. Her husband gathered his family and Sashko and led them back to their ruined flat in the Cheremushki neighbourhood. They spent that night there; in the morning of 18 March they set off from Mariupol in a car whose windows had been blown out by shelling and threaded their way past dozens of Russian checkpoints.

Olena watched those so-called 'liberators' with contempt—a coarse roll call of brutality. There were convicted men, tattoos and all, swearing in criminal slang; there were Buryats, notorious for their cruelty—who, witnesses said, would break into basements, throw in a grenade and bolt the doors so the buildings groaned for days with the wounded trapped inside; and there were plain, ignorant thugs, the self-styled liberators who terrorised the civilian population.

At first the family planned to travel to Yaremche in the Carpathians, where Olena had begun her medical career. In the end they decided to head for France, having heard refugees there would receive help. But twelve-year-old Sashko could not cross the border because he had no papers. He stayed temporarily in Lviv with a relative of the Matyushyns while Olena's family resolved how to care for him.

Over the next two months they obtained the necessary documentation and Olena's sixty-one-year-old husband became Sasha's legal guardian—adoption was impossible under martial law, only guardianship. They still lacked a death certificate for his mother. In August 2022 the Matyushyns returned to Ukraine to sort out custody formalities, and on 1 September 2022 Sashko began school in France.

The boy made it to France. He has now finished two years of collège (middle school) and the first year of lycée. He learned French quickly and speaks it fluently; he has adapted very well.

Recently Olena received a provisional list of those killed in the Drama Theatre from a friend. The name of Olena Kuznetsova—Sashko's mother—appears on it, but there are still no official documents to prove that Sashko is an orphan.

Today Olena has returned to Ukraine and is living in Yaremche to care for her nearly ninety-year-old mother. Many of her former colleagues from the twenty years she worked after graduating from Donetsk Medical Institute are there too. Olena now works as a physiotherapist at the Yaremche Central City Hospital in the Ivano-Frankivsk region, helping Ukrainian defenders and civilians to recover from serious injuries and illnesses.

Sasha is studying in France with Olena's husband, who is taking an active part in the cultural life there. Olena's daughter remains in Yaremche while her husband is serving with the Ukrainian Army.

Sources: Suspilne Ivano-Frankivsk, YouTube May 2025 https://www.youtube.com/watch ?si=mtn3Fl8WmjSv5onY&v=24WIWgvn-x8&feature=youtu.be; Mediazona 29 August 2022, article by Maksym Butchenko https://zona.media/article/2022/08/29/dramteatr

* * *

The Theatre of Death

This account is drawn from an interview on Vilne Radio with an actress who survived the bombing of the Mariupol Drama Theatre. Vira Lebedynska was the theatre's musical director and an actress; she was forced to flee the so-called 'Russian World' twice. For almost thirty years she had worked in a Donetsk theatre, but in 2014, when the Russians arrived, she escaped to Mariupol, then under Ukrainian control. Vira still recalls fondly her years producing Ukrainian musical performances in Donetsk. Yet the self-styled 'liberators' uprooted her life twice—first in

Donetsk, then again in Mariupol—and came dangerously close to taking her life on 16 March 2022. After surviving that dreadful day, she eventually made her way to Uzhhorod in western Ukraine.

The full-scale invasion on 24 February 2022 shattered Vira. It was hard to grasp that Russia had attacked without declaring war. People were told to stay home; many did. For a few days there was still power, gas and water, then everything vanished—no electricity, no heating, no water, and later, no food. Her son urged her to leave the city, but where could she go? Mariupol was her home: her house, her work, her cat. For over a week she slept in a corridor with the cat for company. On 3 or 4 March an air strike struck the entrance to her block. She survived that strike, packed what she could, and moved to the Drama Theatre for safety.

Vira never left the theatre to venture back into the city. The building no longer resembled a temple of the arts—people were sleeping everywhere: in corridors, in offices, on the steps and on the auditorium floor where all the seats had been removed. The broken chairs served as makeshift beds at night. At first everyone ate what they'd brought, but when supplies ran out they began cooking on improvised campfires, using groceries salvaged by volunteers from bombed neighbourhood shops, and melting snow for drinking water. People pooled their efforts, taking turns to cook and clean, and a first-aid post was set up for urgent cases. Vira and Oksana, her former colleague at the theatre, kept a register of arrivals; before long their list exceeded 1,200 people, all waiting for a promised 'green corridor.' With no electricity or reliable communications, volunteers would sometimes hand out single sheets bearing the day's most important news, while a young couple's radio became the focal point for anyone desperate to hear updates.

Russian aeroplanes often roared overhead, on their way to Azovstal where Mariupol's defenders still held out. The noise was deafening; whenever Vira and Oksana heard aircraft approaching they ducked into their tiny office. They had even painted 'CHILDREN' in large white letters across the theatre's entrance, believing the pilots might see it and spare the civilians below.

On the morning the bombs fell they had risen unusually early. Having finished the morning chores by nine, they were sitting in the office when Vira felt the urge to fetch something from the costume shop—but Oksana would not let her go. Vira's cat suddenly arched its back, fur on end, and at that exact moment an aeroplane passed overhead. In the next instant they heard the terrible, falling-bomb sound: 'ooh-ooh-ooh-ooh.'

There was no thunderous blast—only a muted, vacuum-like thud, then plaster began to rain down. People screamed for help. Vira stood frozen in shock. Oksana's husband went to see what had happened; she didn't know how long he was gone. When he returned he said simply, 'The theatre is gone.'

They fled clutching suitcases and papers, stepping over bodies strewn everywhere. Some people cried out from under the rubble, trapped and pleading for help.

Vira's heart sank; there was nothing she could do for so many. Then she saw an adult bent over a child who seemed lifeless. People were pouring out of the shelter and running for the exits—it looked like the apocalypse. Vira had never witnessed anything so terrifying in her life.

After they left the theatre they ran towards the sea, hearing more explosions or the staccato of shelling. When Vira later saw photographs of the building she realised it had been hit again: the first strike had wrecked it, but the second seemed to have burned it to the ground. What felt like twenty minutes of running had in fact taken nearly two hours. People a few streets away only then understood why those fleeing were coated in white plaster. They begged for shelter and a woman by the seafront took them in despite a huge shell crater in her yard and all her windows blown out. With no warm clothes and temperatures around minus ten, they lit a small stove that offered little comfort; Vira spent two nights there. They wanted to leave Mariupol but transport was scarce—Oksana's car had been destroyed and other vehicles were almost impossible to find. For a time they even considered walking along the shore to Berdyansk. At the last moment the house owners lent them an old car, so Vira, her friends, the owners and several other families set off for Zaporizhzhia. Two days later, no one was being allowed to leave the city.

First they went to Berdyansk, already under occupation, where Russians were everywhere. They stayed two days and then pressed on towards Zaporizhzhia, praying only that God would keep them safe. Along the way they saw Red Cross buses that refused to let them through even though a green corridor was supposed to be open. By some miracle they made it to Zaporizhzhia, and when they saw Ukrainian soldiers they knelt and kissed the ground—the happiest moment of their lives. From Zaporizhzhia Vira endured an overcrowded evacuation train that took almost two days to reach Lviv. Her son met her there and she stayed with him until he found a quieter place on a farm with horses where she could settle. Nature and hypnotherapy helped her slowly recover from the horrors of Mariupol, although for nearly a year and a half she suffered panic attacks and bouts of uncontrollable weeping.

Then the director of the Mariupol Drama Theatre called: the company was resuming work in Uzhhorod and he invited her to join. Vira accepted gladly. She now lives in Uzhhorod in a modest hostel room and shares a stage with the Transcarpathian Musical and Drama Theatre; they often tour. A family who had sheltered in the Mariupol theatre—Olena Bila, Igor Kytrysh and their son—survived because they left a few days before the bombing. Two others, Dmitry Murantsev and his girlfriend, also lived through the attack. The director decided the company must not remain silent: from this experience they created the play *Mariupol Drama*, which tells the story of the building from the first days of the invasion up to the moment of the bombing. At first Vira's mind recoiled from returning to that trauma. Every performance felt like another small death; she still finds herself crying on stage. Yet the audience's reaction—the open, searching faces in the stalls—makes it plain that speaking the truth about Mariupol matters. For her company, theatre has become a weapon against the enemy: there may be no building left, but there are people—actors, witnesses—who resist with art.

Now she watches, bewildered and angry, as the occupiers rebuild the theatre in Mariupol. How can they raise a new façade on the bones of the dead and then dance and sing inside it? Even if they call it a theatre, to Vira it should be a memorial. The reconstruction looks like an attempt to erase what happened on 16 March 2022—to replace massacre with myth. She cannot imagine working there; she fears the voices of the lost will not let anyone find peace.

Source: interview by Julia Markulich on Vilne Radio, the Free Radio of Donetsk, 16 March 2025, https://freeradio.com.ua/ru/mu-perestupaly-cherez-tela-pohybshykh-aktrysa-maryupolskoho-dramteatra-podelylas-vospomynanyiamy-o-rossyiskom-avyaudare/

The *200th* (dead in military slang) who came back

Mykola Kobilnyk came from Drohobych in western Ukraine. A sniper in the 3rd Separate Special Purpose Regiment, he fought under the call-sign 'Eneyko' and is the father of four children—three sons and a daughter. Although he lost a foot to a wound, he is back in service and now easily recognised by his 'bear paw', a shaggy fur prosthesis with claws.

As a boy Mykola loved films about Robin Hood and tried to imitate the outlaw. He never robbed the rich to give to the poor, but he did fashion bows, crossbows and arrows out of reeds—which is why he took up archery. He liked the sport for its discreetness: the bow is set up quietly, shoots quietly and is put away quietly. Later he turned to martial arts. Once, while helping to clear the basement of a block of flats that was to become a martial arts school, a coach noticed the agile youngster and likened him to Eney—the Ukrainian take on the Greek Aeneas, hero of Ivan Kotliarevsky's Aeneid. The opening lines run: 'Aeneas was an agile guy, a Cossack full of life, full of the devil, persistent and spry, there was no one like him.' The nickname stuck, and Mykola adopted Eneyko as his call-sign.

Mykola had never pictured himself as a soldier, still less as a officer—he simply loved his country. Above all, he is a Ukrainian patriot: he loves Ukraine with the same fierce devotion he feels for his family. It pains him to see what the Russian invasion has done to his homeland. He has been fighting since 2014, initially serving two years with the 80th Air Assault Brigade in Lviv. Although he savoured the romance of parachute jumps—the moment the canopy opens, the sky spread out beneath you—he had a different ambition: to join the special forces.

In 2016, after a rotation near Schastye, Mykola took a short leave to attend foreign sniper courses in Zhytomyr. He used the opportunity to travel to Kropyvtskyi and ask to join the 3rd Special Operations Regiment, Svyatoslav the Brave. There he met 'Redut', Olexander Trepak, a Hero of Ukraine, and, having passed the demanding psychological and physical tests and obtained a reference from his previous unit, he began the special-forces training. Six months later he was enrolled in the regiment— a great honour he vowed to live up to.

Sniping runs deep in his blood. During his compulsory army service in 1993 he was already a sniper, and before that, as a civilian, he had been an amateur hunter. He knows his rifle intimately: respect and knowledge, he says, make a weapon a friend. Mykola has not let go of that rifle since, and he does not intend to put it down until Ukraine is liberated from the Russian invaders.

On the morning of 24 February 2022, Russia launched its full-scale attack on Ukraine. Columns of Russian forces rolled forward in such huge numbers it felt surreal— like a war in a video game, hundreds of vehicles and tens of thousands of troops.

Mykola managed to evacuate his brothers' families just hours before the occupiers reached the towns and villages of the Kyiv region, shepherding them out of Irpin under fierce shelling. He later learned that many civilians had been killed simply for being relatives of Ukrainian servicemen. The first days and weeks of the invasion were unbearably painful.

After the Kyiv region was liberated, his unit fought at Marinka, Lysychansk, Sievierodonetsk and Bakhmut. The Russians had expected to be welcomed with flowers and bells—instead they met 'Hyacinths', 'Peonies' and other weapons. For Mykola his principal tool of war is a .338-calibre Cadex rifle fitted with a domestically produced ARCHER TSA-7 thermal-imaging system. He also carries a Ukrainian flag—because, he says, that is what the Russians fear most.

Mykola was wounded while on a combat mission in eastern Ukraine—literally one step from death—but, with the help of his brothers-in-arms, he was pulled out of the minefield and kept alive.

It happened during the battles around Sievierodonetsk, after they had crossed the River Donets and taken positions near Lysychansk. Intelligence pointed to an enemy attempt to encircle the town, advancing from several directions. At 05:05 one morning Mykola went out on reconnaissance following an intense artillery barrage that had raked the area. The barrage had carpeted the ground with mines—hundreds of them. In June, dense foliage only made things worse: falling mines would shave off leaves and be hidden by the greenery, and with fierce fighting under way there was no time to search carefully.

Mykola, the first man out that morning, stepped on a mine and it detonated. Over the radio he called, 'Cherry, Cherry—'Eneyko' is a 200th.' Then, to his own astonishment, he realised he could still move a little and corrected himself: 'Stand down. I'm a 300th.' (In military slang '200th'—from the Soviet-era 'Cargo 200'— means dead; '300th' means wounded.)

His brothers-in-arms were on him in minutes. Mykola could not feel his right leg—it was a serious situation—but adrenaline kept him moving. He began to give himself first aid to staunch the bleeding. The danger, though, was everywhere: mines lay not only around him but beneath his head and under his right shoulder. Any wrong movement could have set one off.

Against the odds his comrades managed to extract him from the minefield, painstakingly avoiding further detonations. They applied a tourniquet and impro-vised dressings, carried him to the stabilisation post, and from there he was rushed to hospital. Part of his leg had to be amputated, though the surgeons fought to save what remained of his foot.

Mykola was awake and fully aware of the damage. He understood at once that the foot could not be saved—only a single toe and a fragment of bone remained. His one request to the surgeon was simple and urgent: 'Do it quickly so I can get back to my unit. My brothers are waiting and I need to keep working.' He knew the war was intensifying and that, as a skilled sniper, he had a role to play.

Determined, he set himself a concrete target: return to his unit within six months. Three days after the amputation he was already exercising—push-ups and other routines—pushing through the pain and the phantom sensations. Physical effort became his medicine; by forcing his body to move he dulled the phantom pain and staved off self-pity. When he looked at the stump he gave himself no indulgence: this was not the end of his life but another episode in it. Losing a foot only hardened his resolve. Rather than defeat him, it became fuel—more motivation to live, to recover and to keep fighting.

Mykola insists losing a foot has made him stronger. Of course he would rather have both legs, but that is no reason to lose heart. He trusts in the resilient spirit of the Ukrainian people and believes the world will see it is impossible to defeat Ukraine. Losing a limb is painful and frightening; losing a life is a grief for family and country. But, he says, God forbid we lose Ukraine—that would be irreparable. You can defeat an army, he argues, but you cannot defeat a whole people; trying to do so is like painting the sky—impossible.

While still in hospital after the operation, Mykola happened upon an adver-tisement for a clinic in Minneapolis, Minnesota—the 'Prosthesis Foundation'—offering care to servicemen with amputations. He applied, despite friends urging him to stay: 'Our doctors are skilful,' they said; 'you can get a good prosthesis here.' The more they discouraged him, the more determined he became to see what help might be available so far away.

He posted his application and discovered he was number 400 on the waiting list. The clinic replied, asking why his case should be prioritised. Mykola's answer was plain and urgent: he had to get back to the front as soon as possible; there was no time to wait. He explained his motivation, and, to his surprise, the foundation responded that he would be moved to the front of the queue and requested his medical records. The trip was then coordinated through the Ministry of Health of Ukraine and his military commander.

Back in 2014 Mykola's call sign had been 'Bear Cub'—he even had a real bear paw mounted on a stand at home. When he was fitted for a prosthesis he decided it should echo that emblem: he photographed and filmed the paw and sent the images to Minneapolis. The team there were intrigued and obliged, making him a prosthesis shaped like a bear's paw. Mykola vowed he would march in it at the victory parade in Moscow—as a sign of Ukraine's triumph over the villains from Moscow.

He underwent rehabilitation in the United States where he and other Ukrainian soldiers were fitted with high-quality prosthetic limbs. Taking his first confident steps with the new limb, Mykola shouted, 'Glory to Ukraine! Glory to America! Get ready, you Russian bastards, I am coming for you!'

True to his word, Mykola was back on duty sooner than many expected. Wounded on 22 June 2022, he returned to his unit on 15 October 2022 wearing his new prosthesis. The 'bear paw' is ceremonial—he looks after it carefully and does not wear it every day. His dream remains the same: to march in it at the Ukrainian victory parade.

Mykola returned to service six months after losing his foot and is now actively taking part in combat missions. You can be broken physically but not spiritually. He fights not because he wants to kill, but because he must defend his homeland, his family and his children—to hand on a free, prosperous Ukraine to future generations. That is his strongest motivation.

He sees what Russia brings: death, the destruction of towns, the killing of children, the elderly and women, and a broader destabilisation of Europe and the world. That must be stopped. Mykola believes with all his heart that the Ukrainian Army and the Ukrainian people are more than capable of doing it.

Sources: interview 8 April 2025 for Army TV (Armiya TV—Ukraine's military TV channel) https://armyinform.com.ua/2025/04/08/dvohsotyj-yakyj-povernuvsya-nejmovirna-istoriya-bijczya-enejka/; https://lviv.cx.ua/drohobychanyn-boiets-sso-z-vedmezhoiu-lapoiu-zmahavsia-u-ihrakh/; https://drohobych-rda.gov.ua/news/nezlamnyy-navit-z-protezom-yak-zakhysnyk-z-drohobychchyny-prokhodyt-reabilitatsiyu-v-amerytsi.html

Two remarkable elderly people: Lidia Galyadzinova from Chasiv Yar and Petro Rohach, a veteran of the Second World War

Lidia Galyadzinova is a 97-year-old IDP from Chasiv Yar in Donetsk region who, in 2025, had been living in a shelter in Kramatorsk for two years because fighting still rages in her native town. In truth she is 98—her mother subtracted a year from her age in 1942 to try to spare her deportation to a labour camp in Germany. As a girl she helped the war effort in the Second World War, carrying water and whatever else was needed to the factory when Soviet soldiers were in Chasiv Yar.

The second war of her life, the one Russia imposed on Ukraine in 2022, forced her to flee the house and the graves she had tended for years. Russian forces—some 10,000 troops, according to the account—took Chasiv Yar and her home was destroyed by shelling; she had hidden in the basement while the bombardment went on and on, and finally accepted evacuation by volunteers. Lidia was an accountant by training and worked for sixty years; it pains her to think of the three-room flat with its two TVs and good furniture that is gone. She left with only a suitcase and a bag, but she managed to save a few clothes and the precious photographs of her great-grandchildren, which she proudly shows to the interviewer.

Her relatives live far away—in the UK and Australia—and they phone constantly, begging her to join them. But Lidia refuses. Above all, she wants to be buried in Chasiv Yar beside the eight members of her family; the thought of resting in a foreign cemetery, among strangers, is unbearable to her.

Volunteers look after her at the shelter, yet Lidia strives not to be a burden. She insists on managing as much of the daily routine as she can: cleaning, cooking, washing the floor and doing the dishes, even though one leg aches badly. She uses a cane and a walker but still finds things to help with, and she takes pride in keeping the shelter spotless—it reminds her of the immaculate apartment she maintained for decades while raising four children. Her one remaining dream is simple and fierce: to return to Chasiv Yar and to see her great-grandchildren again.

*   *   *

Petro Rohach, a 97-year-old Second World War veteran, is now an internally displaced person because of the Russian invasion. At the time of his interview in 2025 he had been living in a regional shelter for six months. Petro comes from Myrnograd, a frontline town in Donetsk region where fighting began in 2024; the front line now lies just 1.5 km from the city.

Forced to leave his home once more, he took with him only a few precious things: old wartime photographs and his soldier's coat, still bearing his orders and medals—including one 'For the liberation of Ukraine' and a certificate listing the liberated cities. All his relatives are now either in Russia or in occupied Ukrainian territory, so the shelter has become his home and the staff and fellow displaced people his new family. After everything he has endured, Petro says the shelter feels like the kingdom of heaven.

Petro was born on Reshetylove farm in Zaporizhzhia region. As a young man during the Second World War he was deported to Germany for forced labour, together with dozens of other Ukrainian youths, including his best friend Mykola from the same village. The two of them managed to escape and went on to serve in the Soviet Army at the age of 17. Petro served in heavy artillery and worked as a scout for his regiment on the front; he was wounded in Czechoslovakia but was fortunate to reach hospital and survive. After demobilisation he settled in Myrnograd, worked for many years in the local mine and raised a family. His friend Mykola died some 15-20 years ago. Today Petro has no hope of returning to Myrnograd—once a clean, comfortable town, it has been razed to the ground—so he savours each day he is given.

Sources: interviews in Suspilne Donbas, 1 June 2025, https://suspilne.media/ donbas/1030315-ne-hocu-v-avstraliu-97-ricna-pereselenka-z-casovogo-aru-zive-u- selteri-kramatorska-istoria/ (Lidia Galyadzinova) and 5 May 2025, https://suspilne. media/donbas/1010263-vtrativ-dim-cerez-drugu-vijnu-u-zitti-istoria-97-ricnogo- veterana-drugoi-svitovoi-petra-rogaca-z-mirnograda/ (Petro Rohach)

Epilogue

The people whose voices fill these pages endured what should never have been endured. Their voices are their truth, and they echo the experiences of many others who, across time, have experienced the scourge of war.

Since the invasion began, millions have been displaced, thousands killed, and urban spaces reduced to rubble. Yet from basements, captivity, and exile, Ukrainians continue to affirm the same truth: that freedom is non-negotiable. Some may find the extracts in this book overly patriotic, but they are also stubbornly brave. With many drawing parallels between Churchill and Zelensky, one wonders whether, with time, the chant "never surrender" will become part of a future Ukrainian narrative of victory.

To frame this book within a broader historical and literary tradition, we recognise that many important previous works have captured the human cost of war in different contexts. During the Soviet period, much of the Ukrainian experience was absorbed into a wider Soviet narrative. Vasily Grossman, a Ukrainian writer who served with the Red Army during the Second World War, documented his experiences on the Eastern Front. His writings, collected in *A Writer at War* (Beevor & Vinogradova, eds. and trs.), reveal the moral and emotional toll of war. *The Unwomanly Face of War* by Svetlana Alexievich gave voice to Soviet women, many of them Ukrainian, whose experiences in the Second World War had long been silenced. Catherine Merridale's *Ivan's War* is perhaps one of the most comprehensive studies on the theme and offers insight into the lives of ordinary Soviet soldiers during the Second World War, many of whom were Ukrainian.

Ukrainian War Stories continues this tradition. Jenny and Nadiia have done an excellent job of translating and compiling the words of civilians, soldiers, prisoners, and survivors. Each story is an act of remembrance. The stories gathered here belong not only to Ukraine but to the shared memory of a world still struggling to understand what war does to human beings.

The testimonies show us that every account follows a similar pattern: destruction, survival, witness. Their experiences have value, and each person remembered preserves a fragment of truth, and together the book forms a record for posterity.

Tony Garcia and Max Lauker